FOR ORGANS, PIANOS & ELECTRONIC KEYBOARDS

195

HIGH SCHOOL MUSICAL

CW00802610

ISBN 978-1-4234-6512-6

All images and artwork © Disney Enterprises, Inc.

Walt Disney Music Company

DISTRIBUTED BY

HAL•LEONARD®
CORPORATION

7777 W. BLUEMOUND RD. P.O. BOX 13819 MILWAUKEE, WI 53213

In Australia Contact:
Hal Leonard Australia Pty. Ltd.
4 Lentara Court
Cheltenham, Victoria, 3192 Australia
Email: ausadmin@halleonard.com.au

E-Z Play® Today Music Notation © 1975 by HAL LEONARD CORPORATION

E-Z PLAY and EASY ELECTRONIC KEYBOARD MUSIC are registered trademarks of HAL LEONARD CORPORATION.

Visit Hal Leonard Online at
www.halleonard.com

CONTENTS

Now or Never

Registration 4
Rhythm: Dance or Rock

Words and Music by Matthew Gerrard
and Robbie Nevil

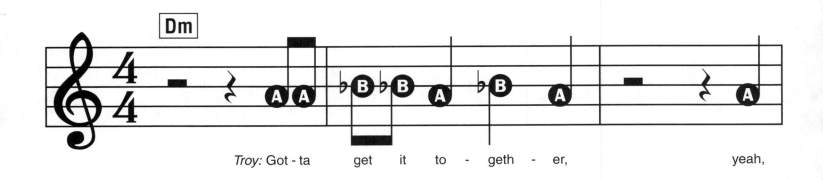

Troy: Got - ta get it to - geth - er, yeah,

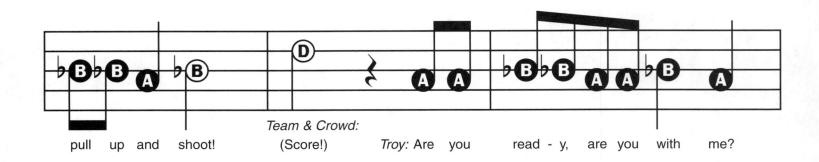

pull up and shoot! *Team & Crowd:* (Score!) *Troy:* Are you read - y, are you with me?

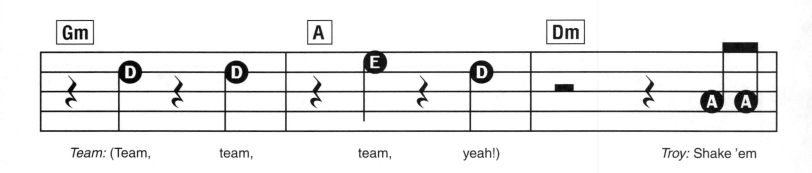

Team: (Team, team, team, yeah!) *Troy:* Shake 'em

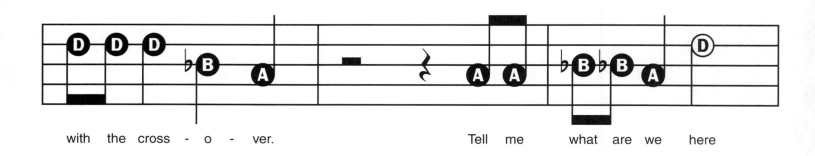

with the cross - o - ver. Tell me what are we here

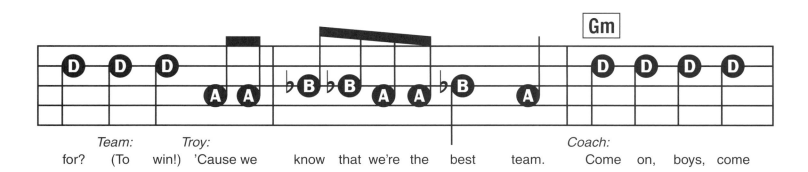

Team: *Troy:*
for?   (To   win!)   'Cause we   know   that   we're   the   best   team.   *Coach:* Come   on,   boys,   come

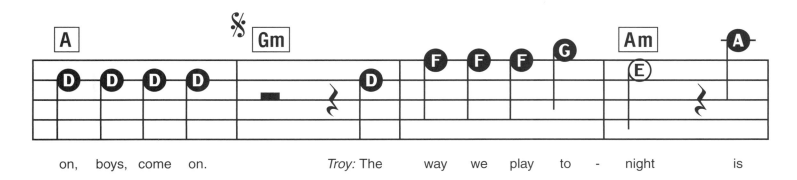

on,   boys,   come   on.   *Troy:* The   way   we   play   to - night   is

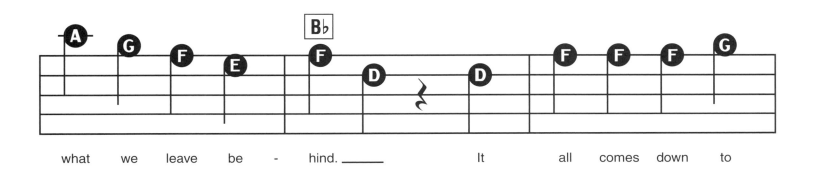

what   we   leave   be - hind. _____   It   all   comes   down   to

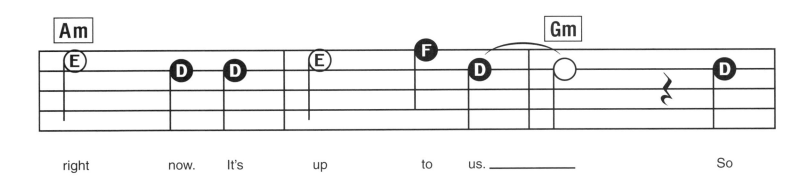

right   now.   It's   up   to   us. _____   So

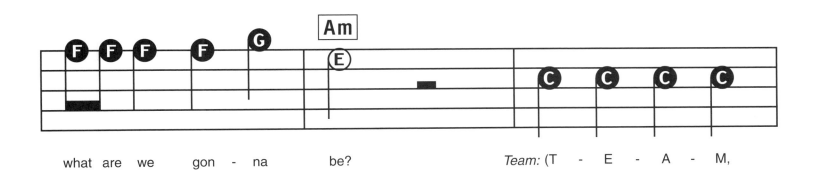

what   are   we   gon - na   be?   *Team:* (T - E - A - M,

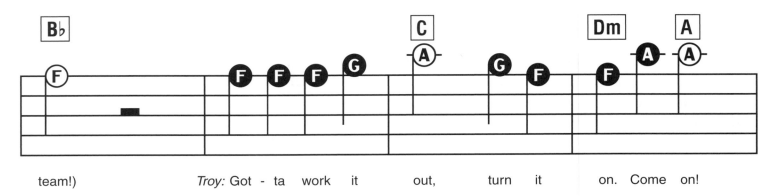

team!)   *Troy:* Got - ta work it out, turn it on. Come on!

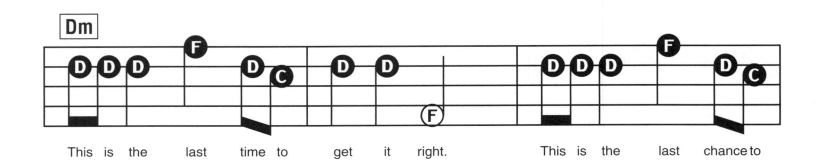

This is the last time to get it right. This is the last chance to

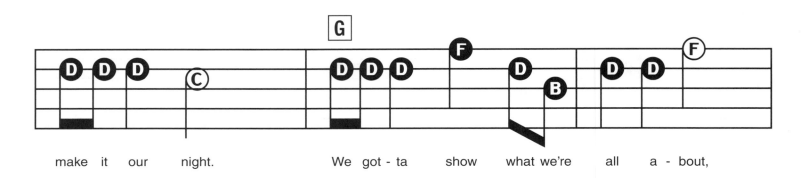

make it our night. We got - ta show what we're all a - bout,

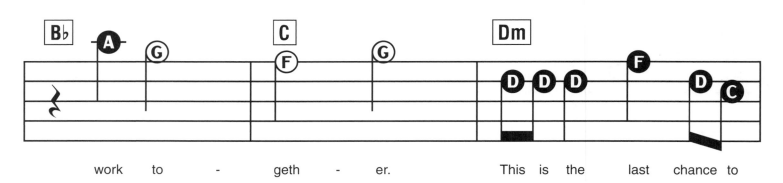

work to - geth - er. This is the last chance to

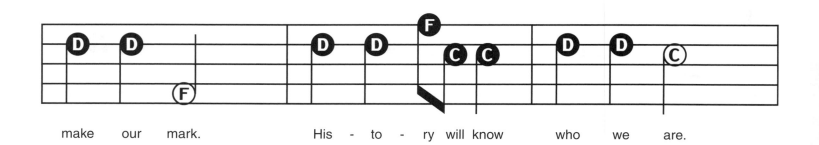

make our mark. His - to - ry will know who we are.

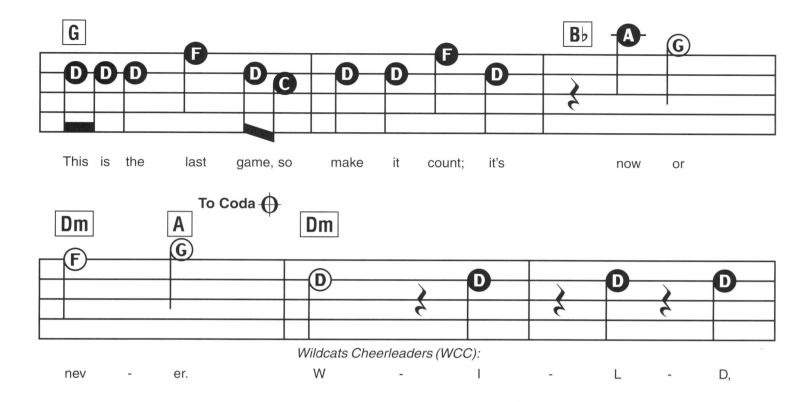

This is the last game, so make it count; it's now or

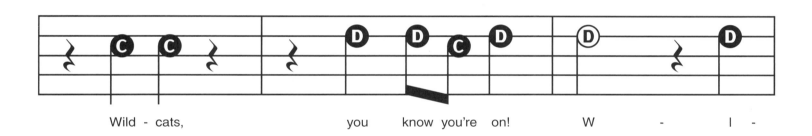

nev - er.   *Wildcats Cheerleaders (WCC):*
W - I - L - D,

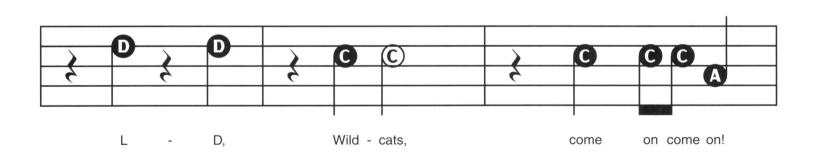

Wild - cats,   you   know you're on!   W - I -

L - D,   Wild - cats,   come   on come on!

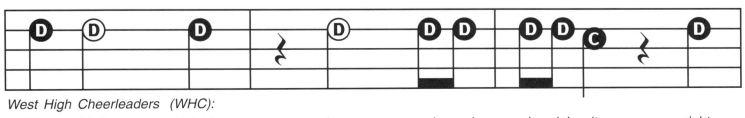

West High Cheerleaders (WHC):
West   High   Knights,   hey,   yeah, we're   do - in'   it   right,

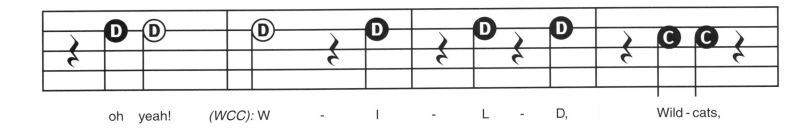

oh yeah! *(WCC):* W - A - I - L - D,   Wild - cats,

now's   the   time.   *Troy:* Got - ta   get   it   in - side,   down   low,

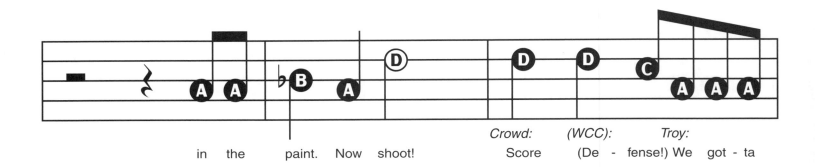

in   the   paint.   Now   shoot!   *Crowd:*   *(WCC):*   *Troy:* Score   (De - fense!) We   got - ta

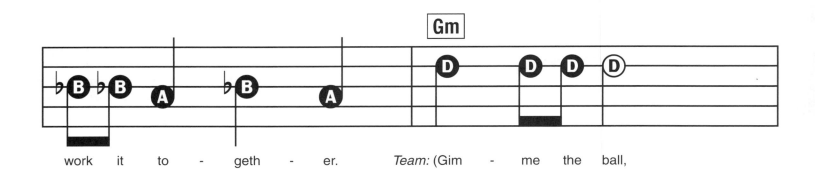

work   it   to - geth - er.   *Team:* (Gim - me   the   ball,

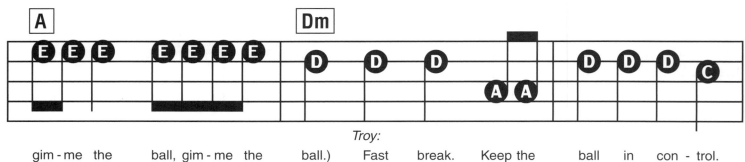

gim - me   the   ball, gim - me   the   ball.) Fast   break.   Keep   the   ball   in   con - trol.

Troy:

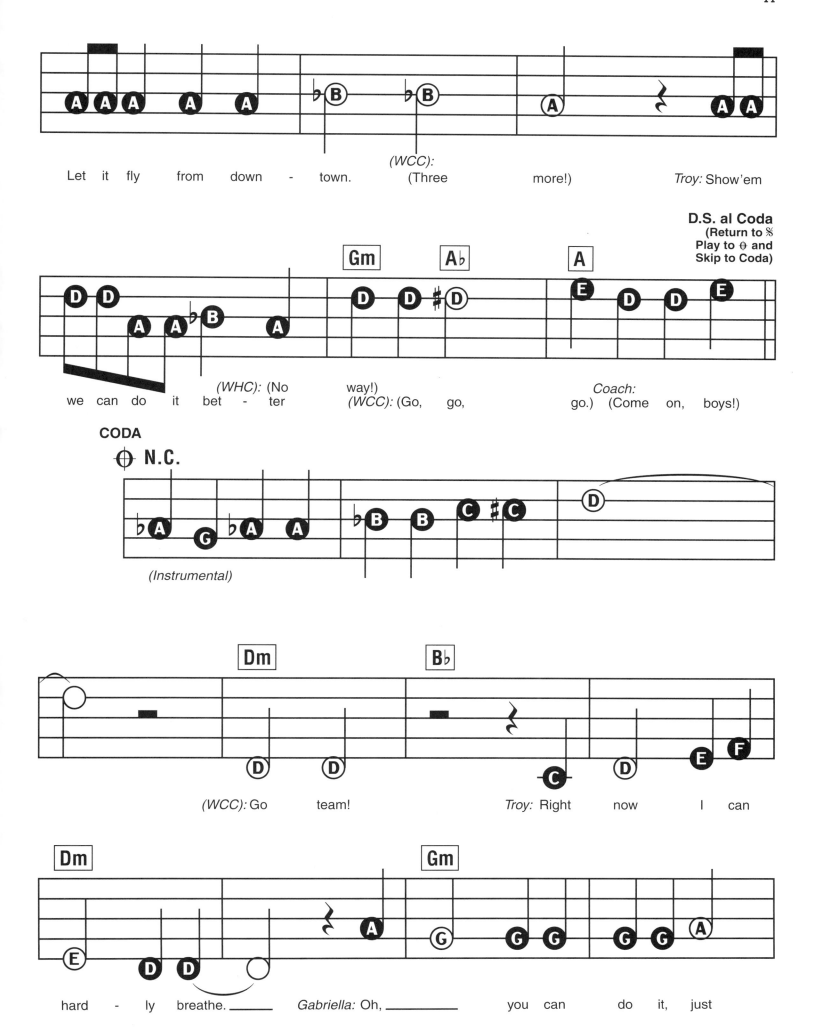

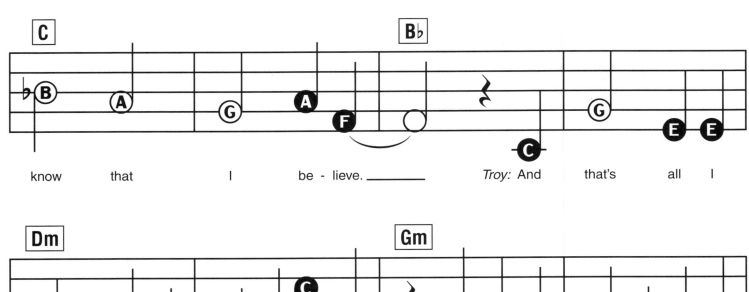

know that   I   be - lieve. _____   *Troy:* And   that's   all   I

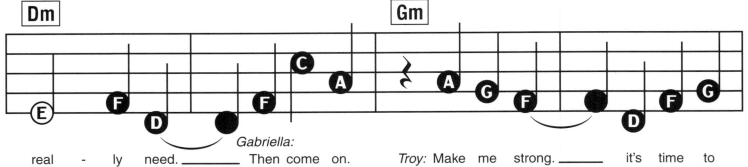

real - ly   need. _____ Then come on.   *Troy:* Make me strong. _____ it's time to

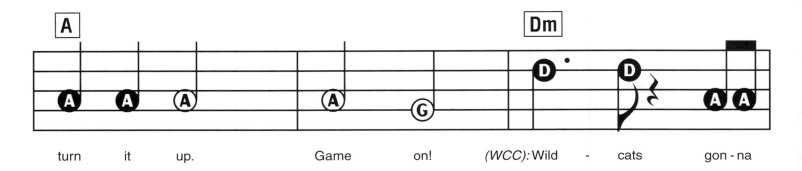

turn   it   up.   Game   on!   *(WCC):* Wild - cats   gon - na

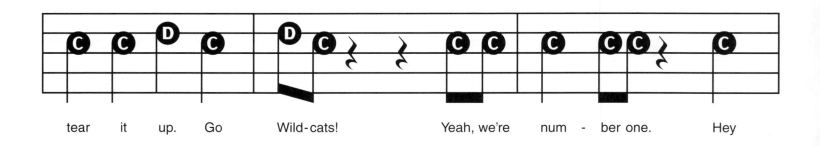

tear   it   up. Go   Wild-cats!   Yeah, we're   num - ber one.   Hey

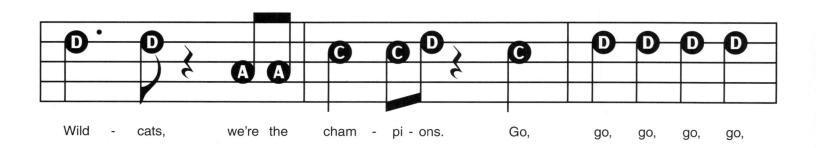

Wild - cats,   we're the   cham - pi - ons.   Go,   go,   go,   go,   go,

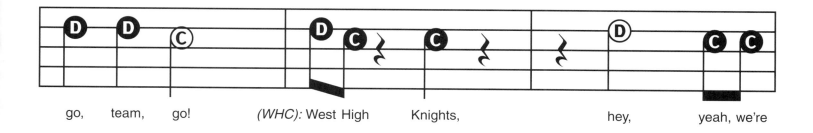

go, team, go! *(WHC):* West High Knights, hey, yeah, we're

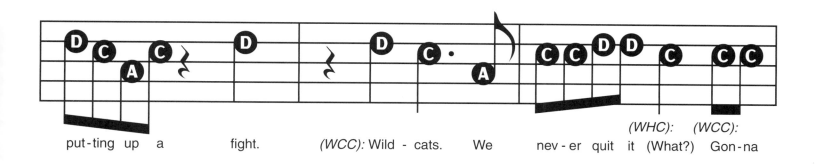

put-ting up a fight. *(WCC):* Wild - cats. We nev - er quit it (What?) Gon-na

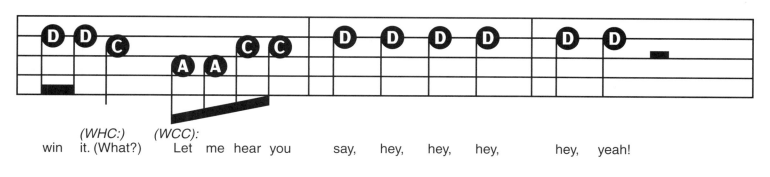

win it. (What?) Let me hear you say, hey, hey, hey, hey, yeah!

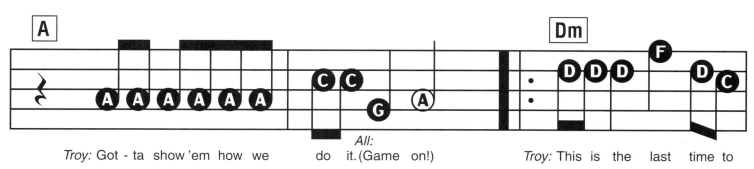

Troy: Got - ta show 'em how we do it. (Game on!) *Troy:* This is the last time to

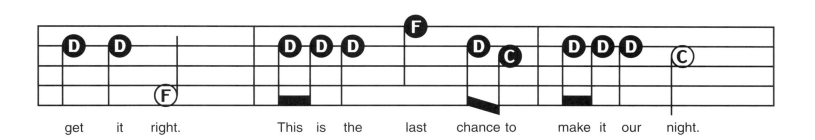

get it right. This is the last chance to make it our night.

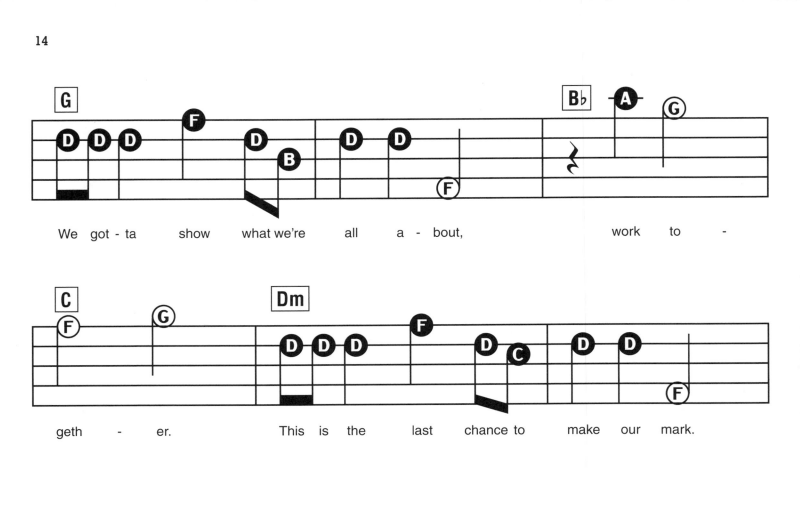

We got - ta   show   what we're   all   a - bout,   work   to -

geth   -   er.   This   is   the   last   chance to   make   our   mark.

His - to - ry   will know   who   we   are.   This   is   the   last   game, so

make   it   count;   it's   now   or   nev - er.

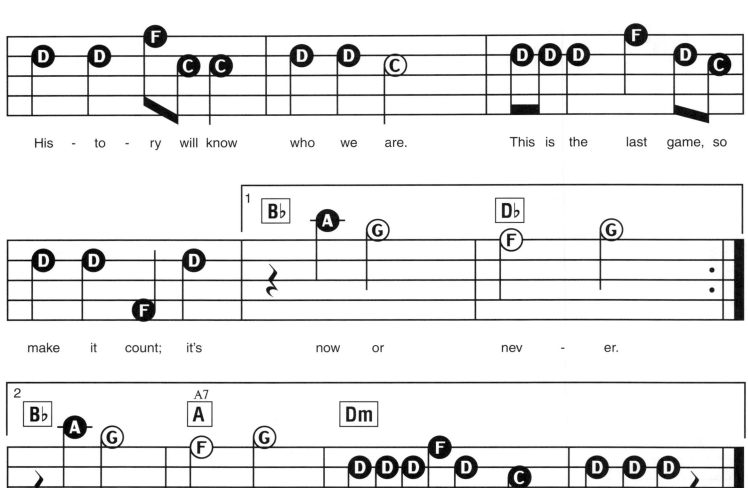

now   or   nev - er.   (Instrumental)

Right Here Right Now

Registration 1
Rhythm: 8 Beat or Rock

Words and Music by
Jamie Houston

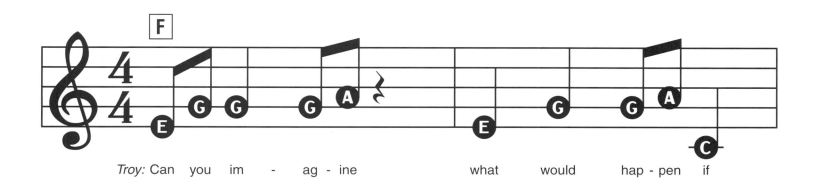

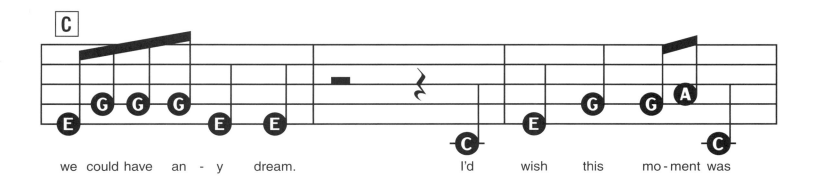

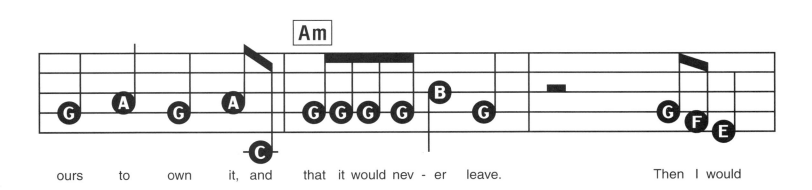

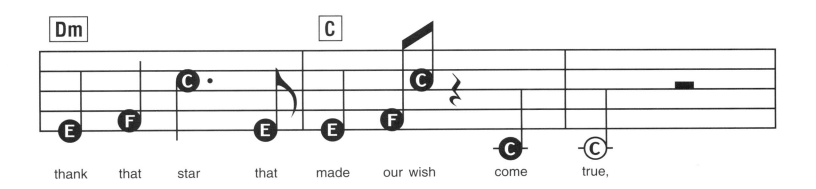

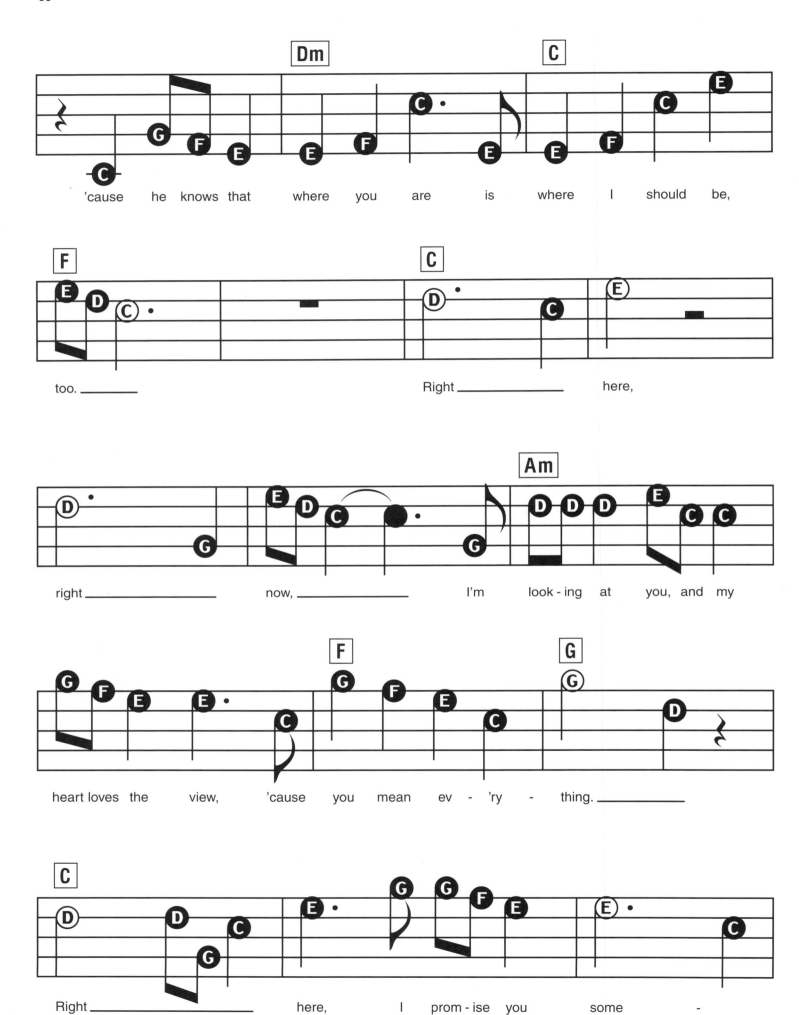

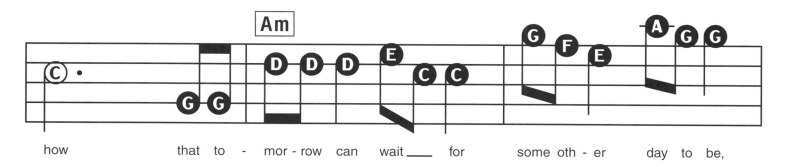

how that to - mor - row can wait ___ for some oth - er day to be,

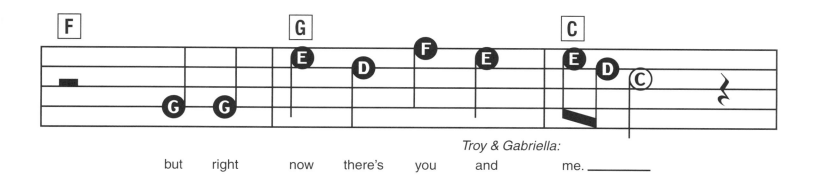

Troy & Gabriella:

but right now there's you and me. _____

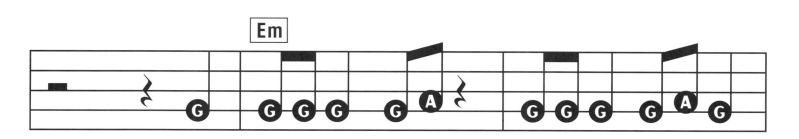

Gabriella: If this were for - ev - er, what could be bet - ter? We've

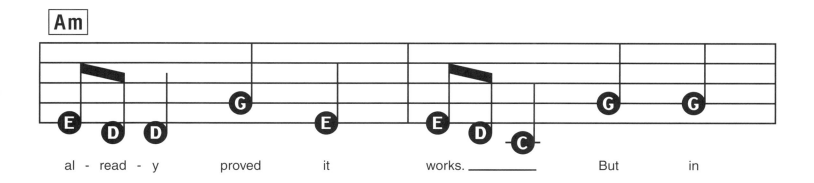

al - read - y proved it works. _____ But in

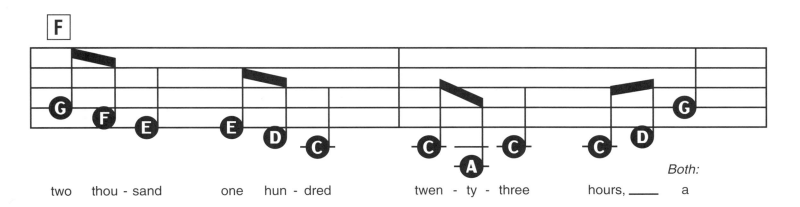

Both:

two thou - sand one hun - dred twen - ty - three hours, ___ a

18

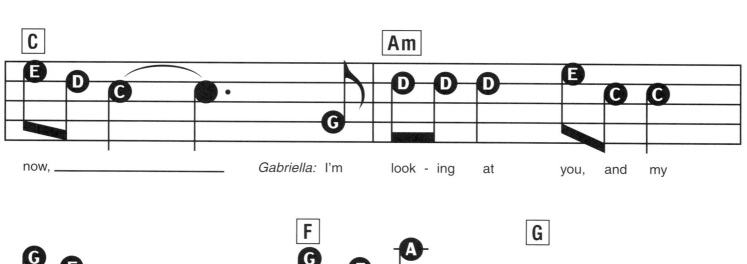

now, _____ *Gabriella:* I'm look - ing at you, and my

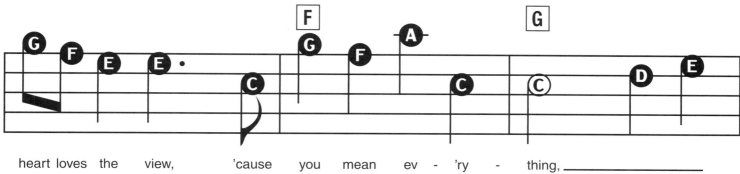

heart loves the view, 'cause you mean ev - 'ry - thing, _____

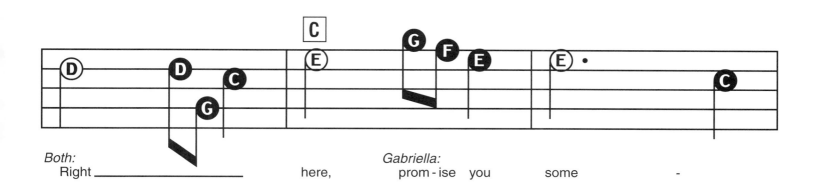

Both:
Right _____ here, *Gabriella:* prom - ise you some -

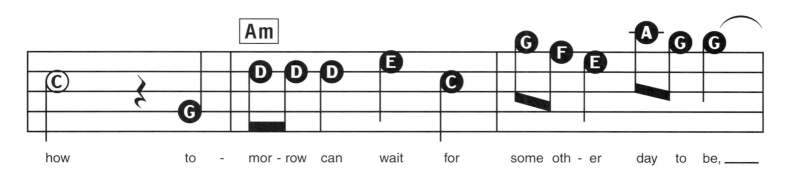

how to - mor - row can wait for some oth - er day to be, _____

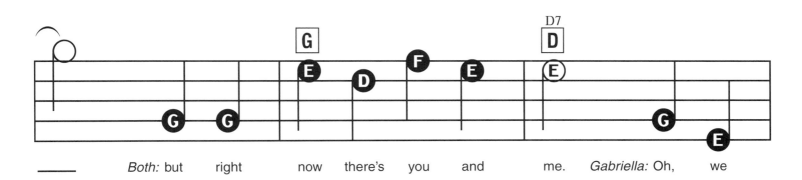

_____ *Both:* but right now there's you and me. *Gabriella:* Oh, we

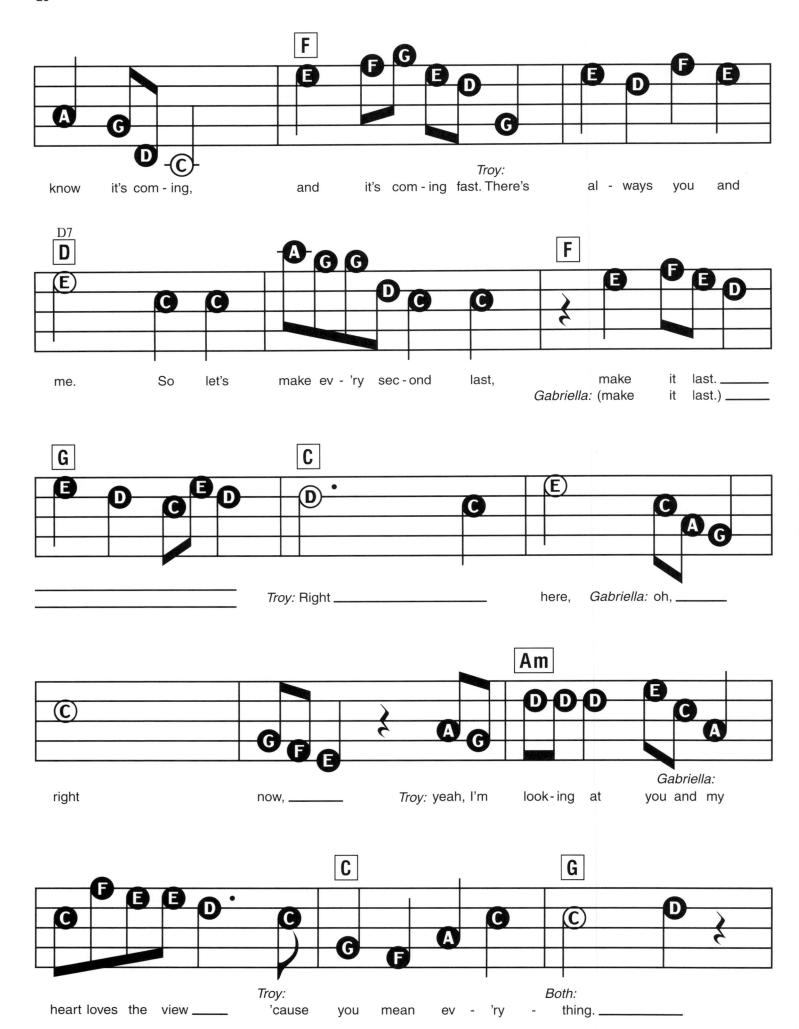

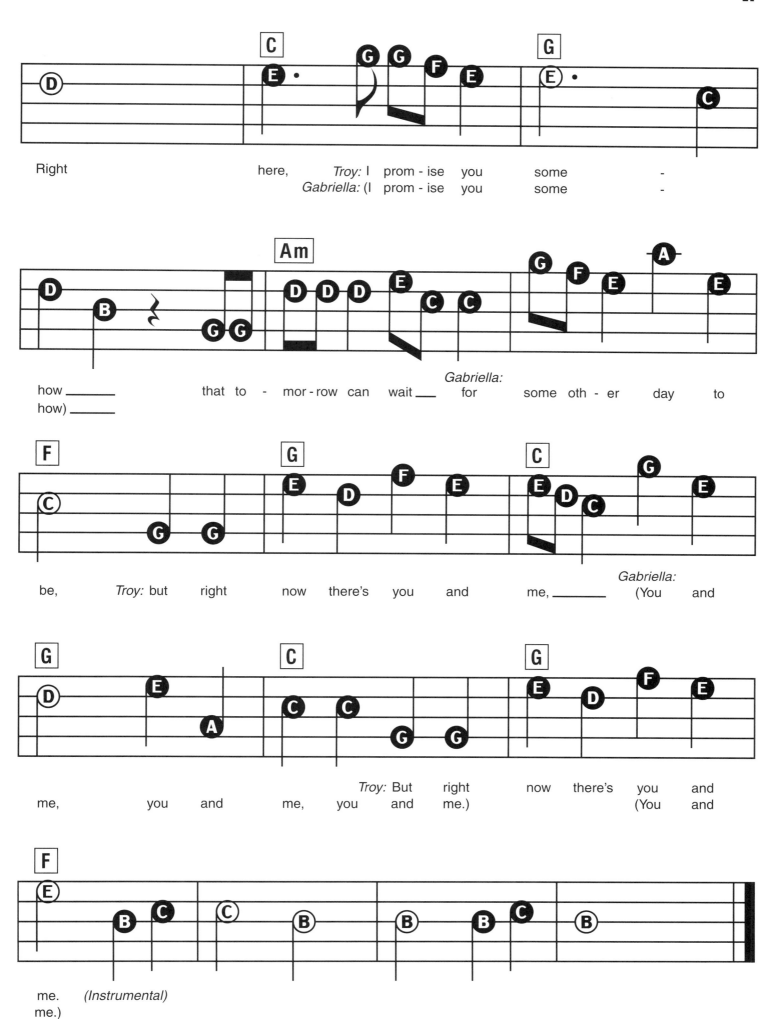

I Want It All

Registration 7
Rhythm: 8 Beat or Rock

Words and Music by Matthew Gerrard
and Robbie Nevil

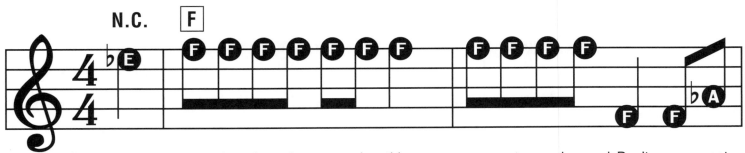

Sharpay: I - mag - ine hav - ing ev - 'ry - thing we ev - er dreamed. Don't you want

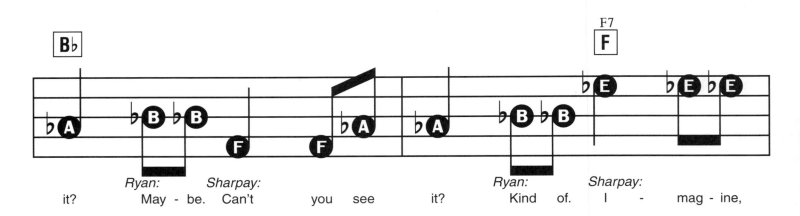

it? *Ryan:* May - be. *Sharpay:* Can't you see it? *Ryan:* Kind of. *Sharpay:* I - mag - ine,

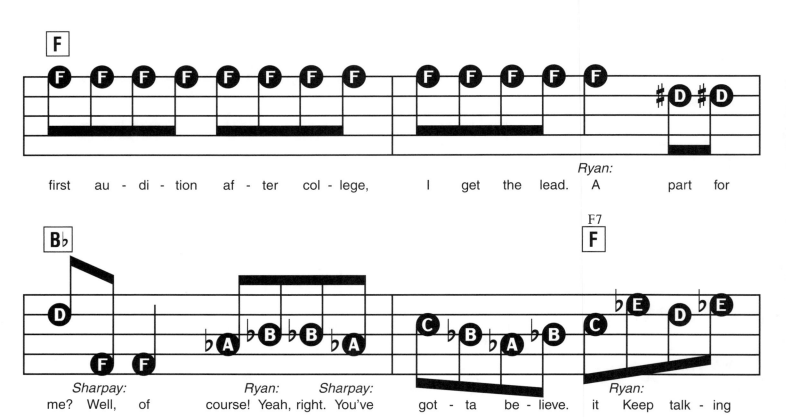

first au - di - tion af - ter col - lege, I get the lead. *Ryan:* A part for

me? *Sharpay:* Well, of *Ryan:* course! *Sharpay:* Yeah, right. You've got - ta be - lieve. it *Ryan:* Keep talk - ing

23

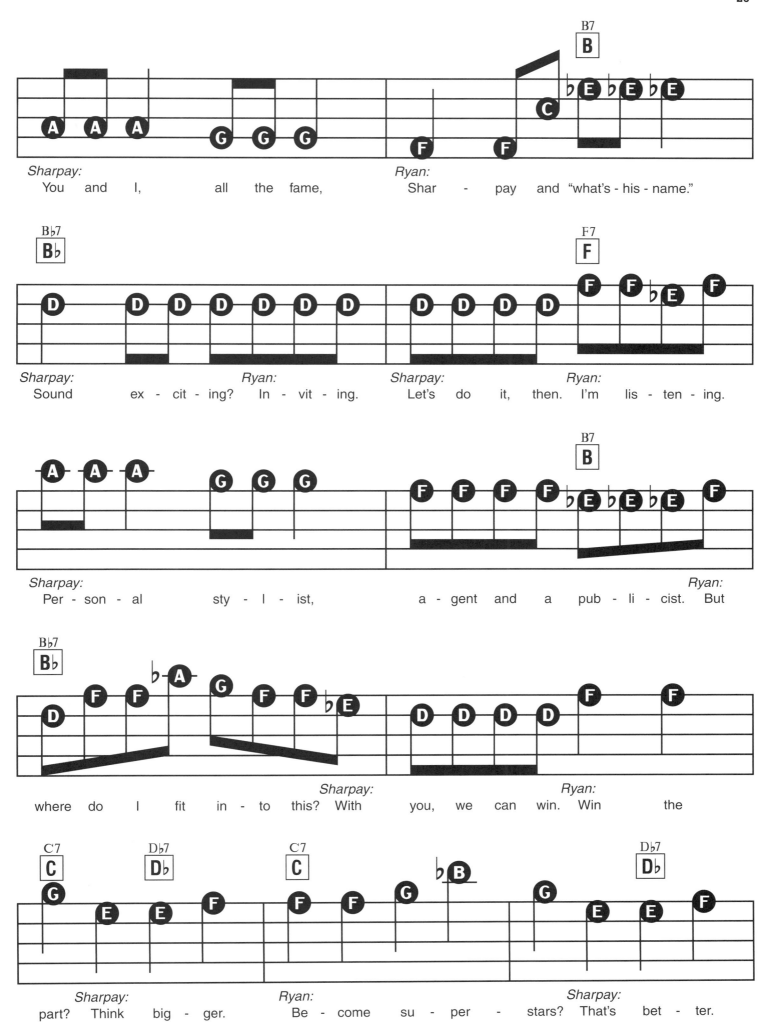

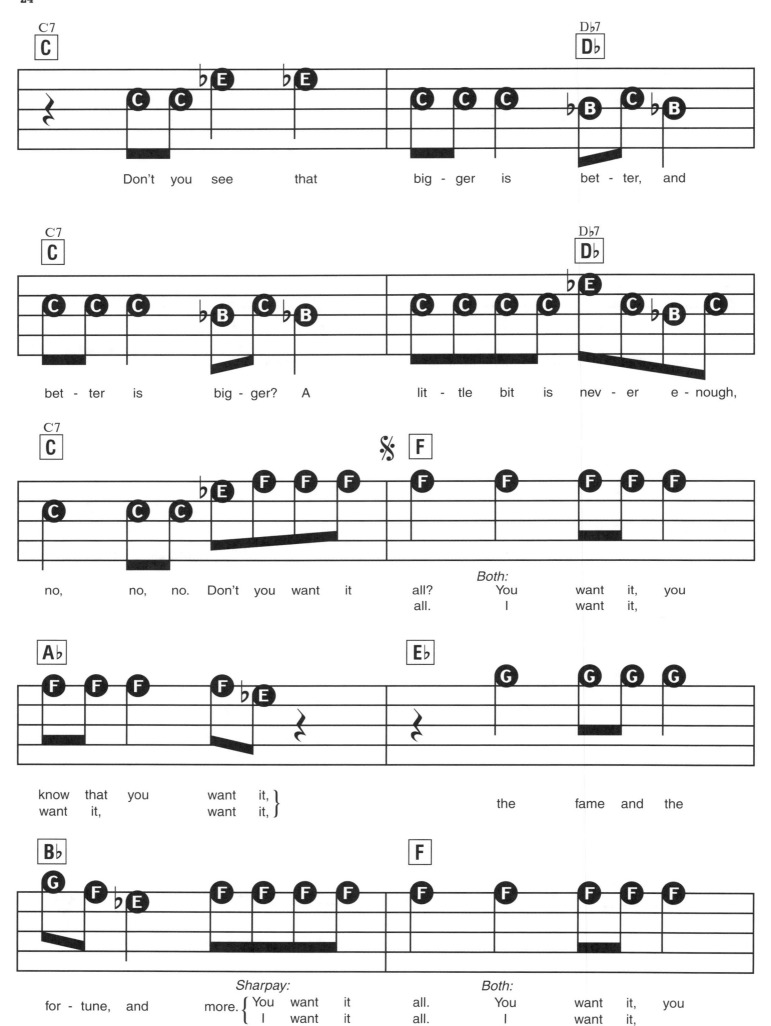

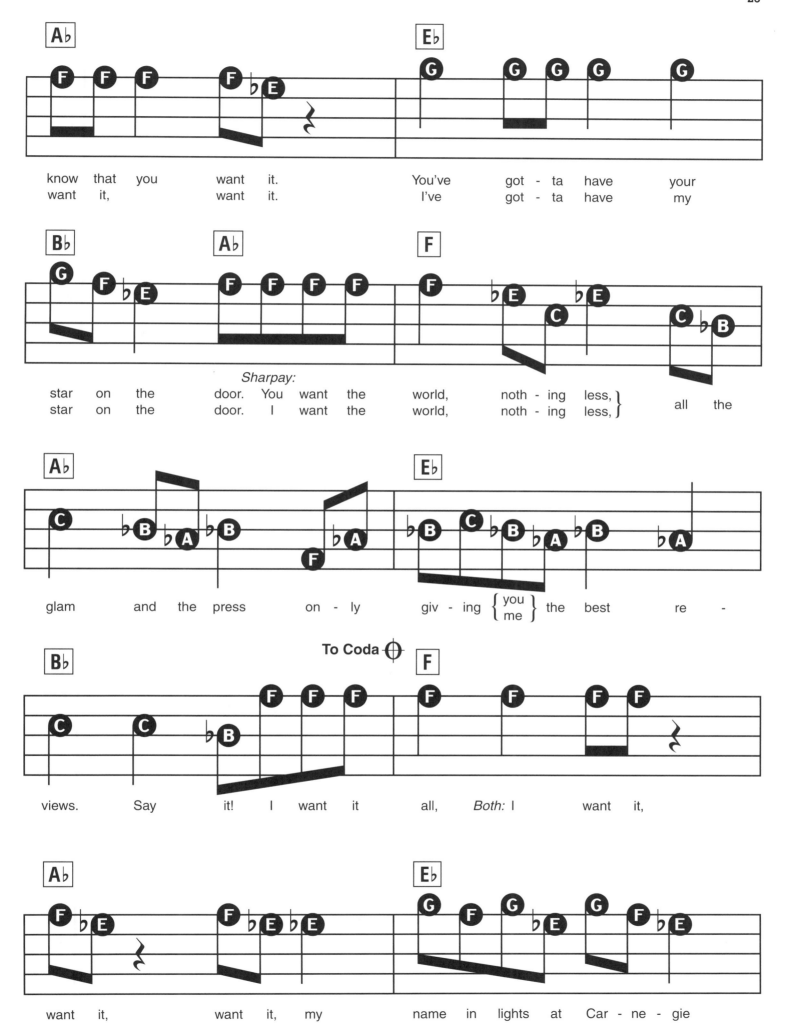

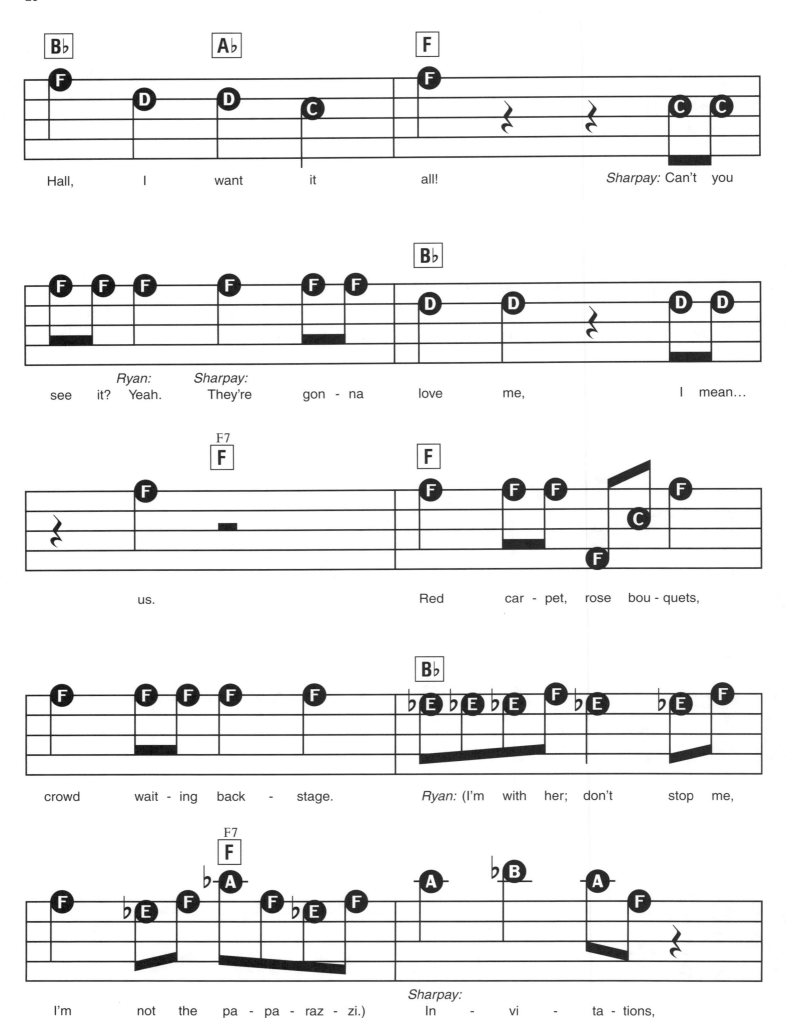

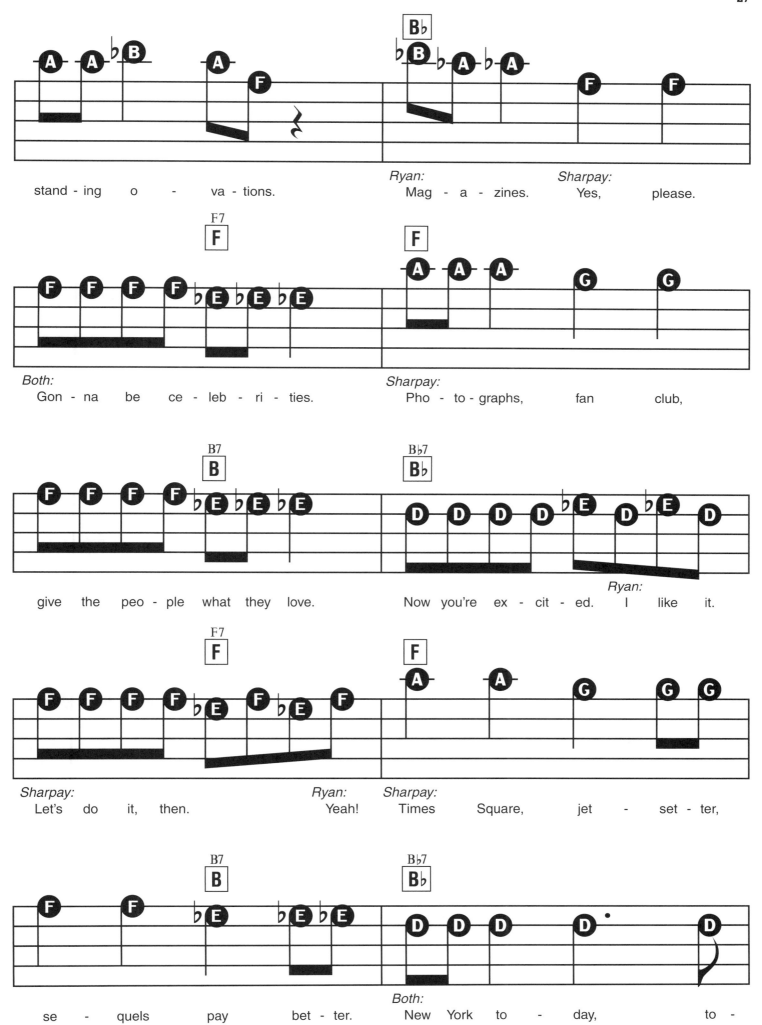

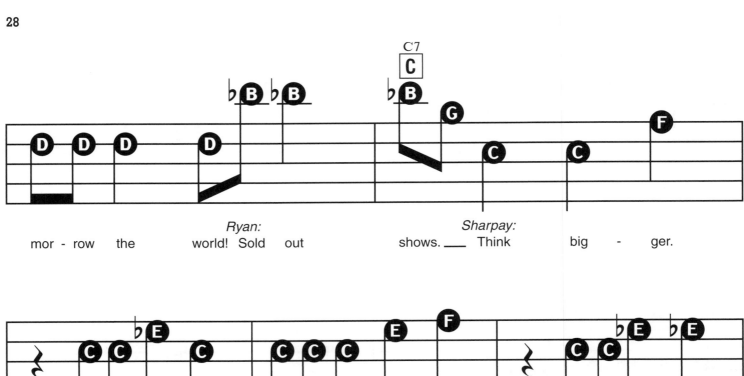

C7

Ryan:
mor - row the world! Sold out

Sharpay:
shows. ___ Think big - ger.

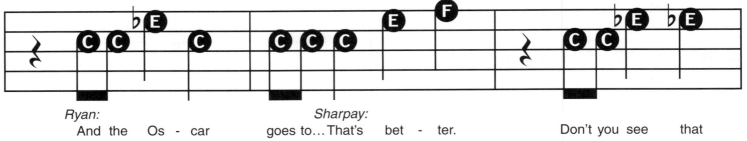

Ryan:
And the Os - car

Sharpay:
goes to... That's bet - ter.

Don't you see that

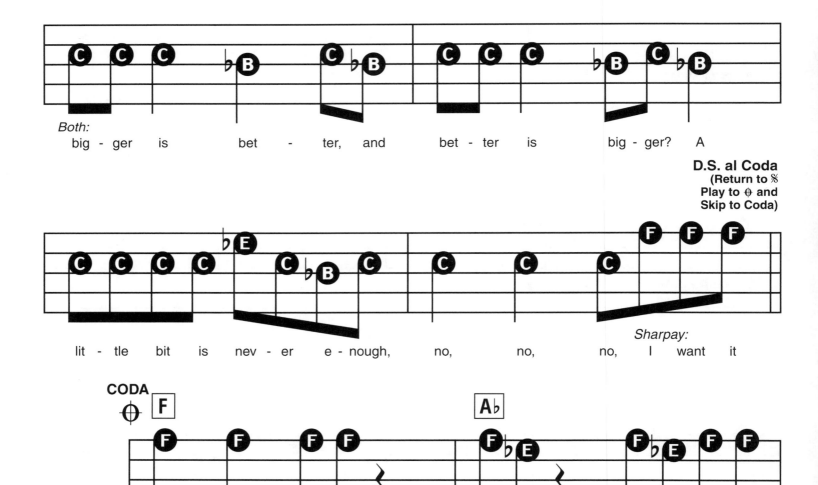

Both:
big - ger is bet - ter, and bet - ter is big - ger? A

D.S. al Coda
(Return to ℅
Play to ⊕ and
Skip to Coda)

lit - tle bit is nev - er e - nough, no, no, no, I want it

CODA
F

Ab

Sharpay:

Both:
all, I want it, want it, want it, Ra - di -

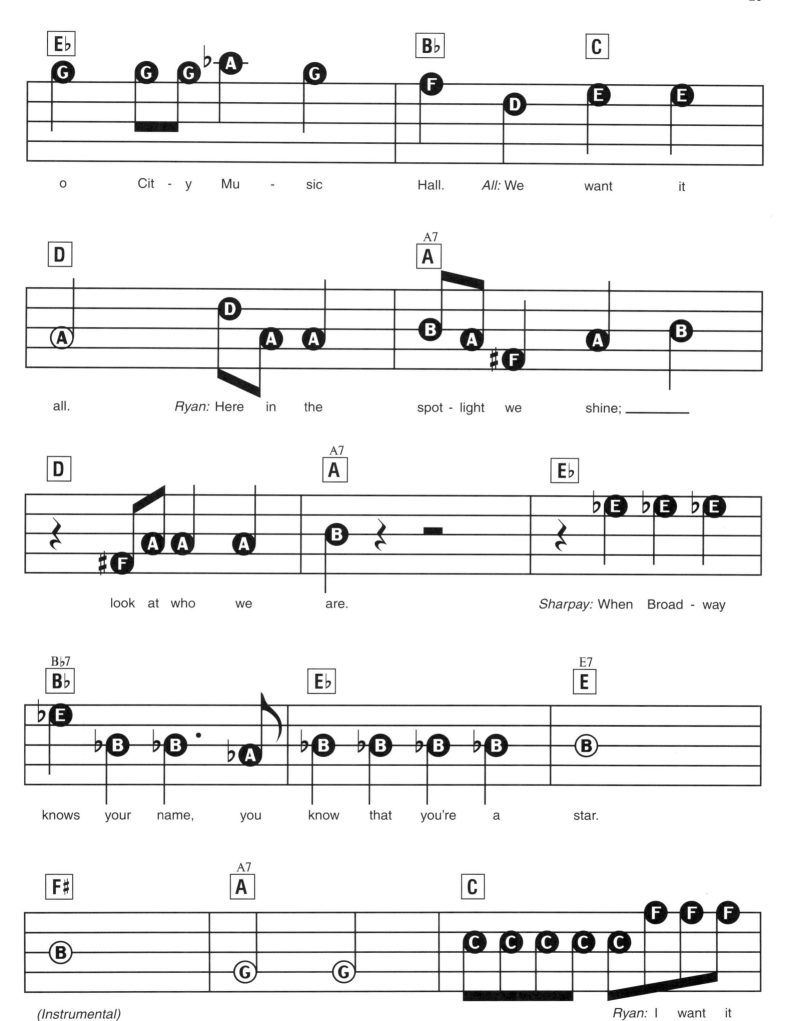

30

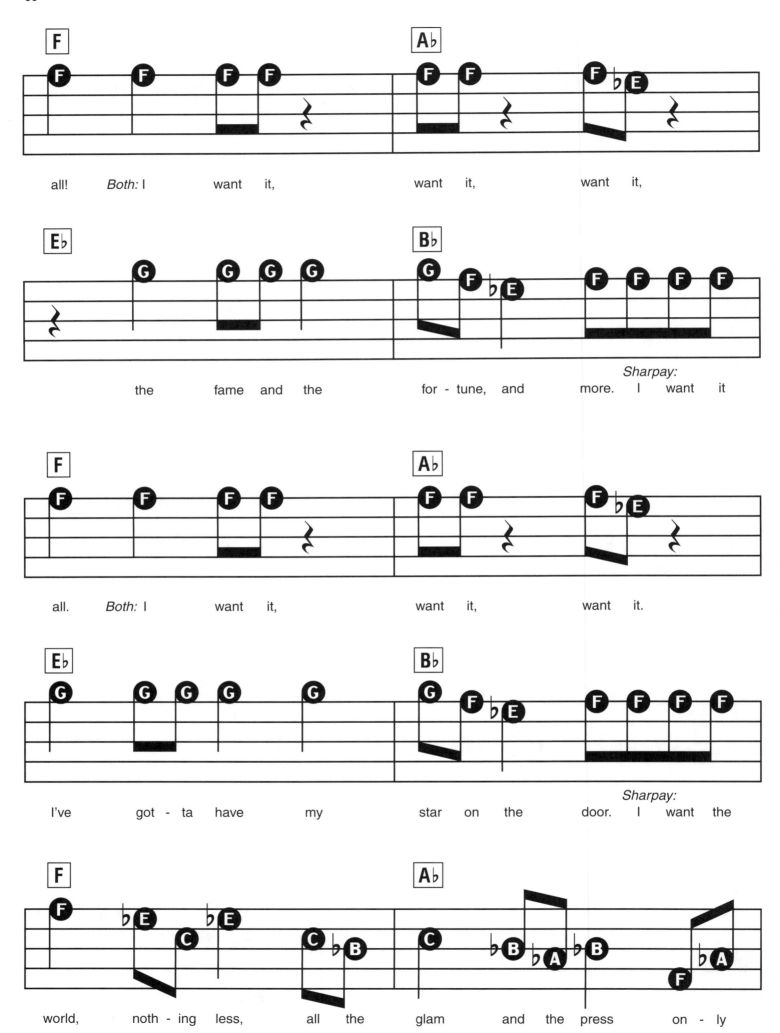

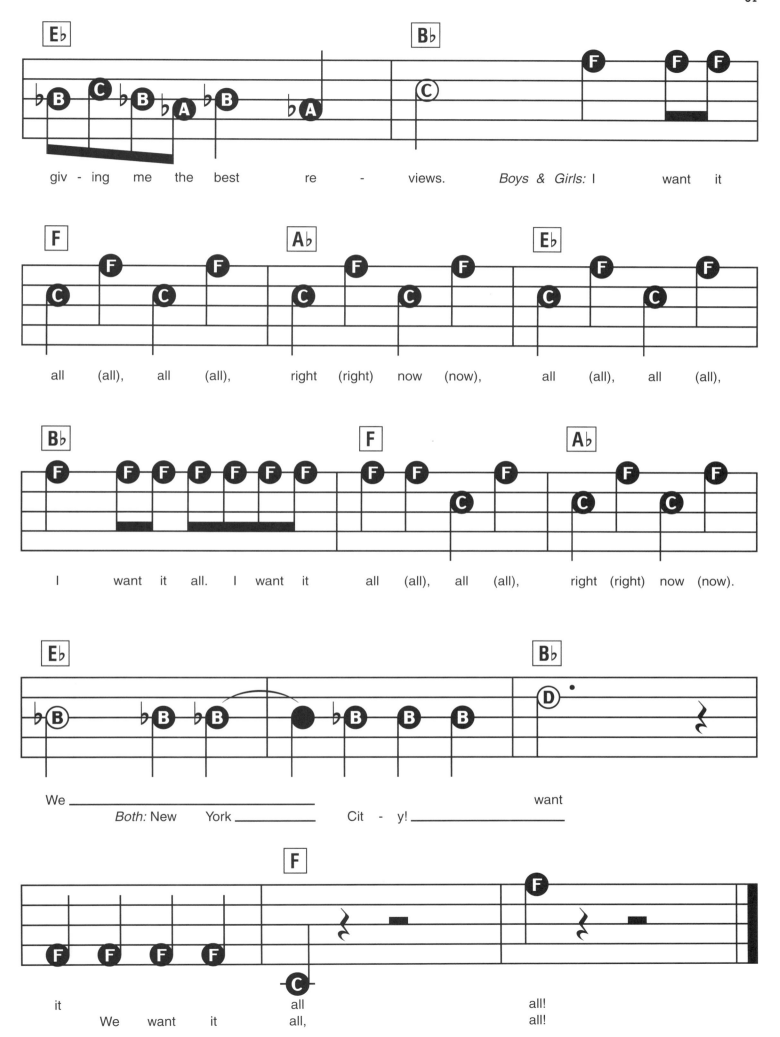

Can I Have This Dance

Registration 2
Rhythm: Waltz

Words and Music by Adam Anders
and Nikki Hassman

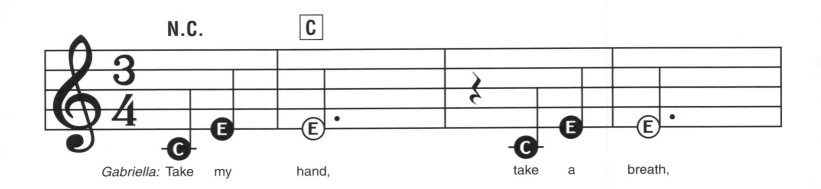

Gabriella: Take my hand, take a breath,

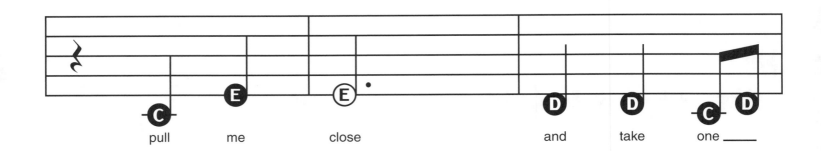

pull me close and take one ____

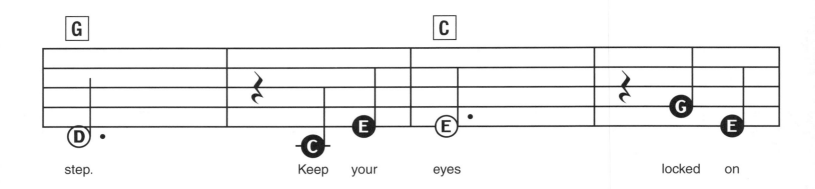

step. Keep your eyes locked on

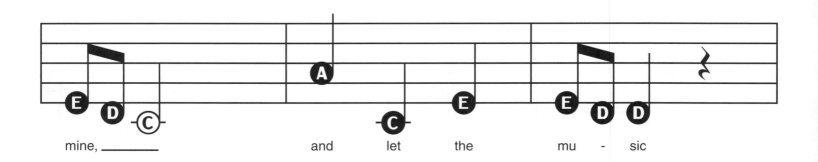

mine, ____ and let the mu - sic

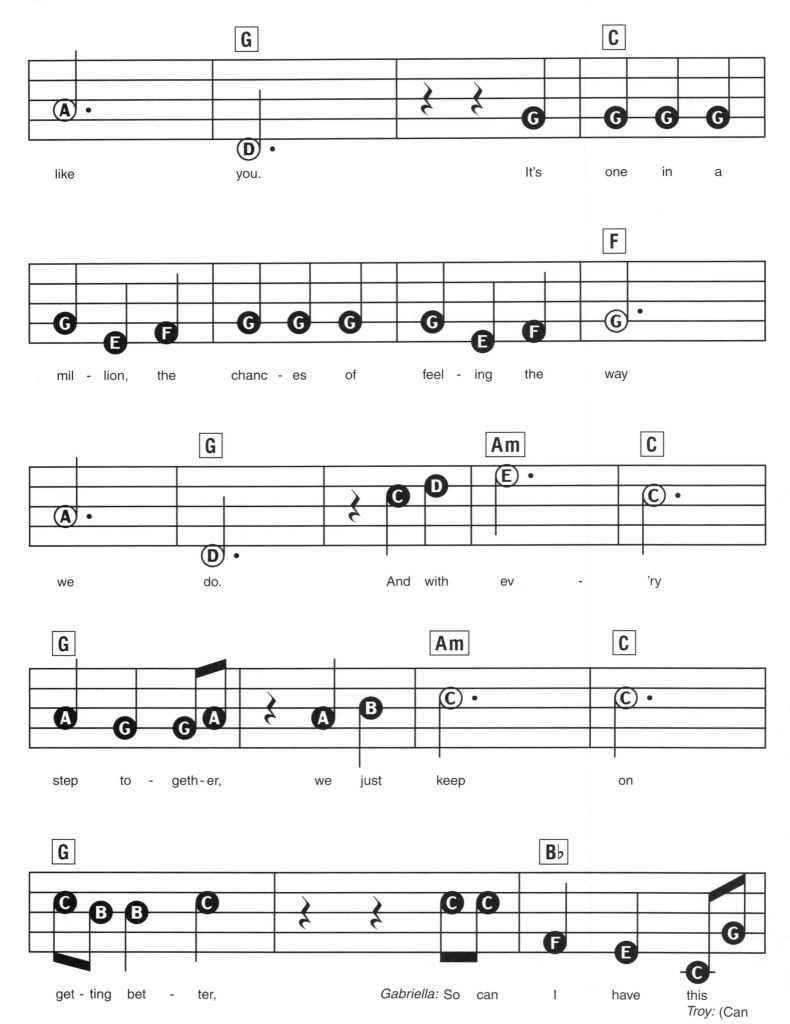

35

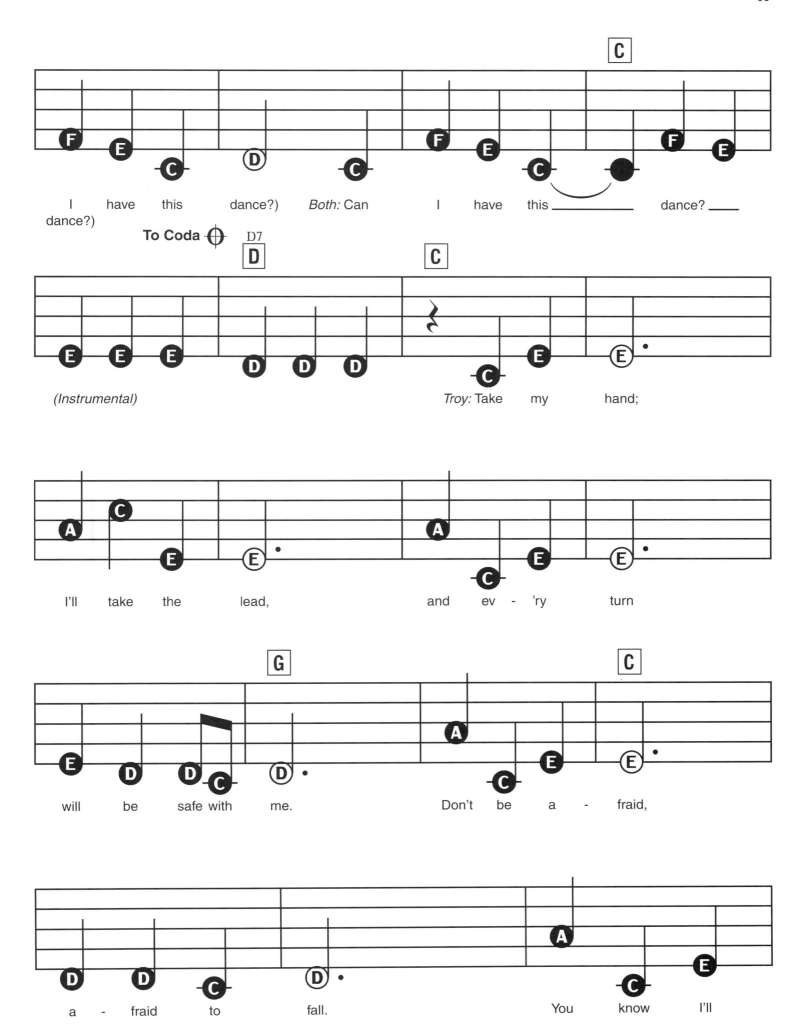

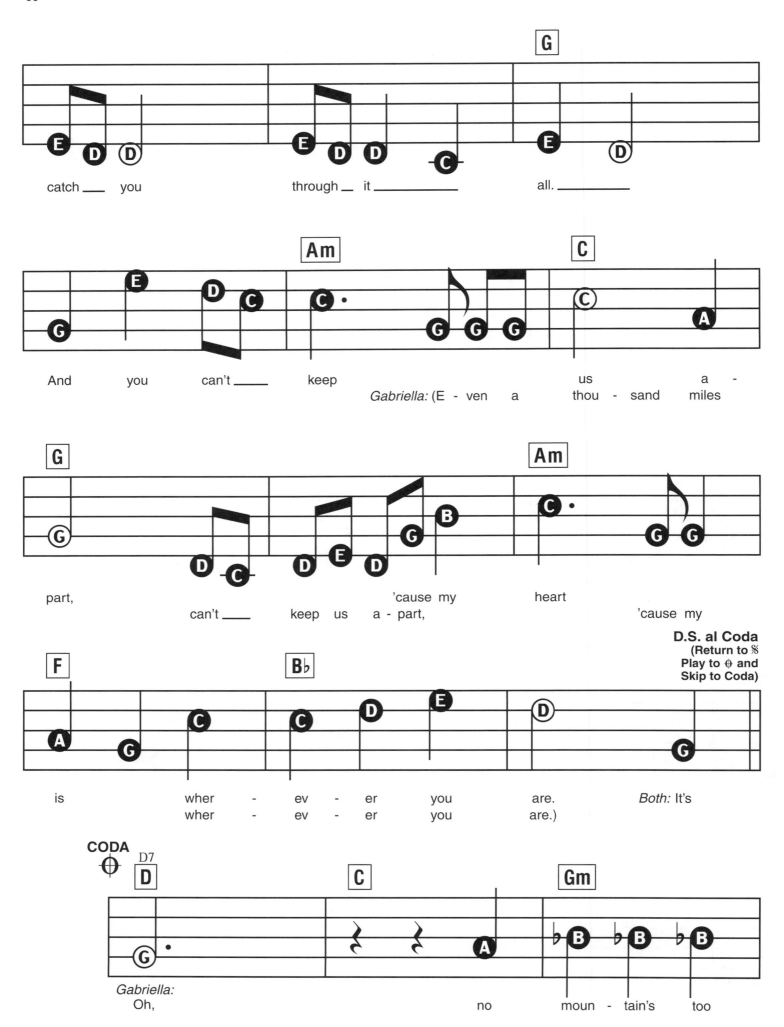

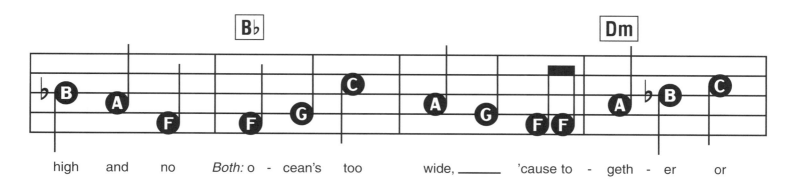

high and no *Both:* o - cean's too wide, _____ 'cause to - geth - er or

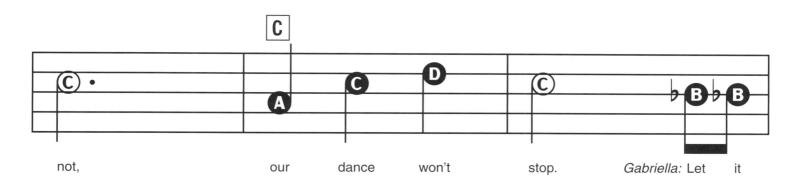

not, our dance won't stop. *Gabriella:* Let it

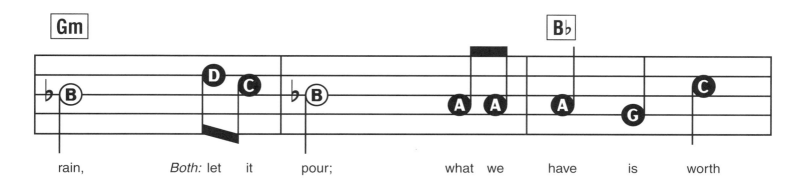

rain, *Both:* let it pour; what we have is worth

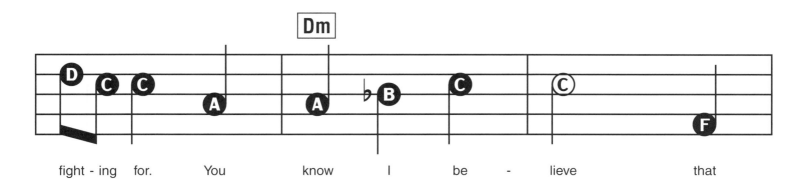

fight - ing for. You know I be - lieve that

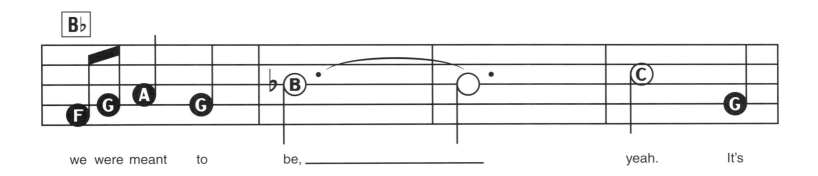

we were meant to be, _____ yeah. It's

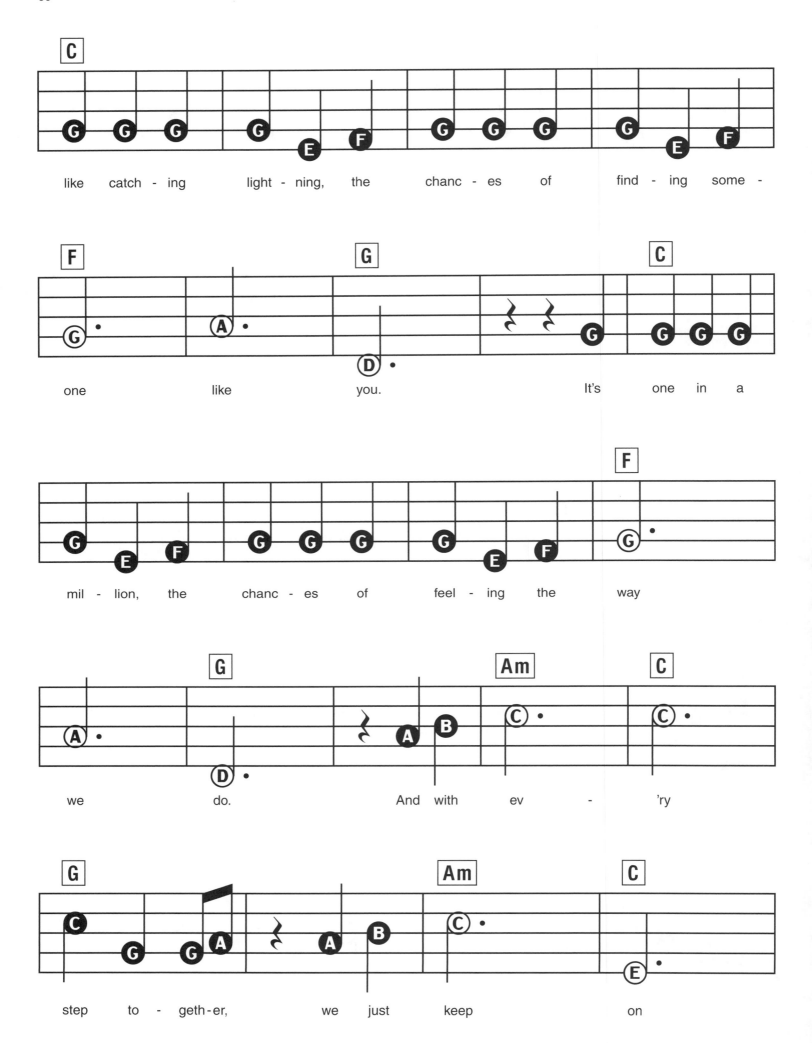

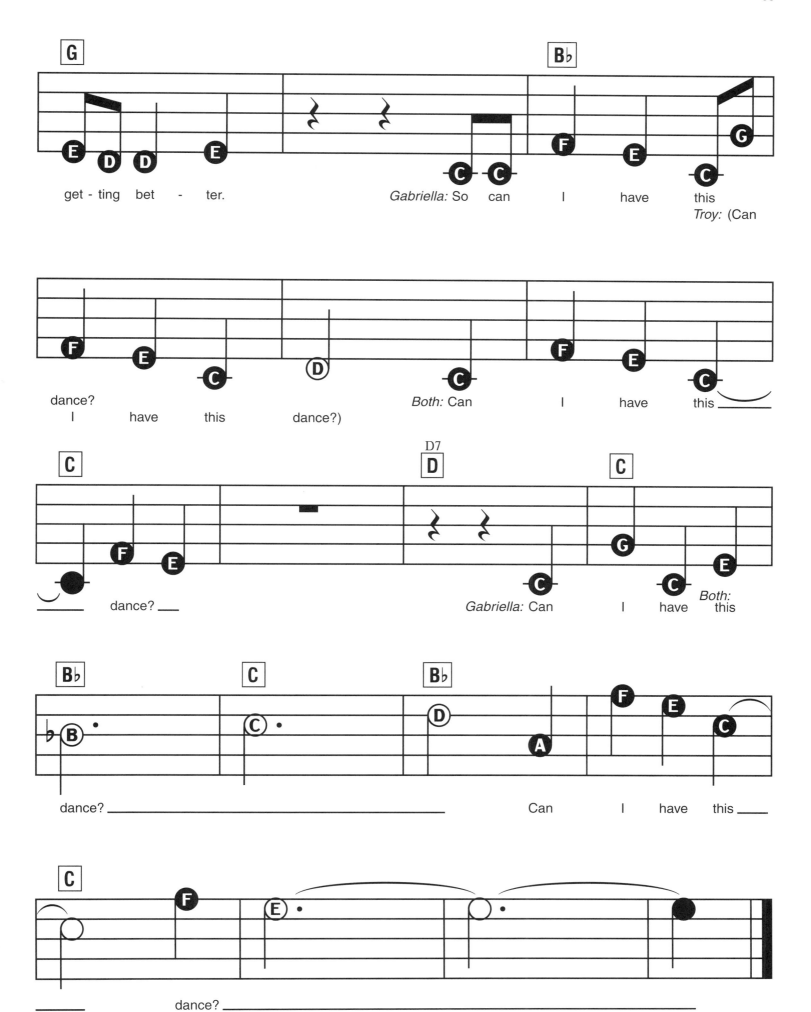

Just Wanna Be with You

Registration 8
Rhythm: 8 Beat or Rock

Words and Music by Andy Dodd
and Adam Watts

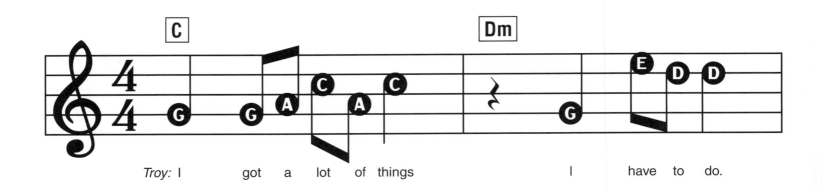

Troy: I got a lot of things I have to do.

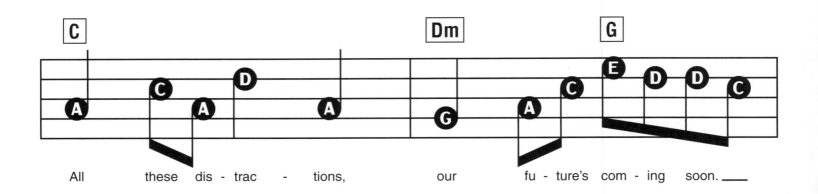

All these dis-trac-tions, our fu-ture's com-ing soon.___

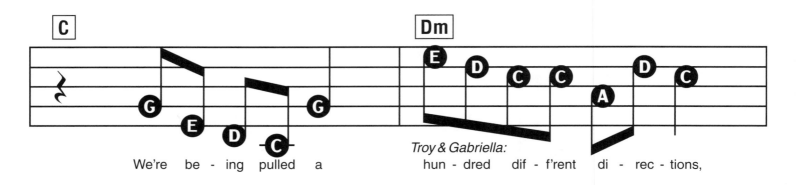

We're be-ing pulled a

Troy & Gabriella: hun-dred dif-f'rent di-rec-tions,

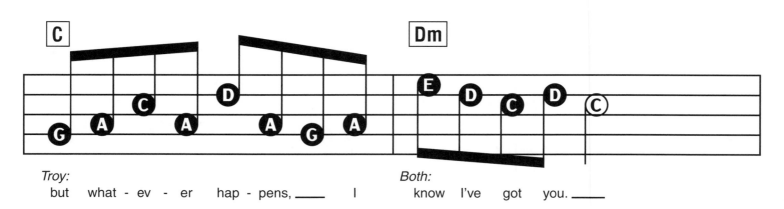

Troy: but what-ev-er hap-pens,___ I

Both: know I've got you.___

41

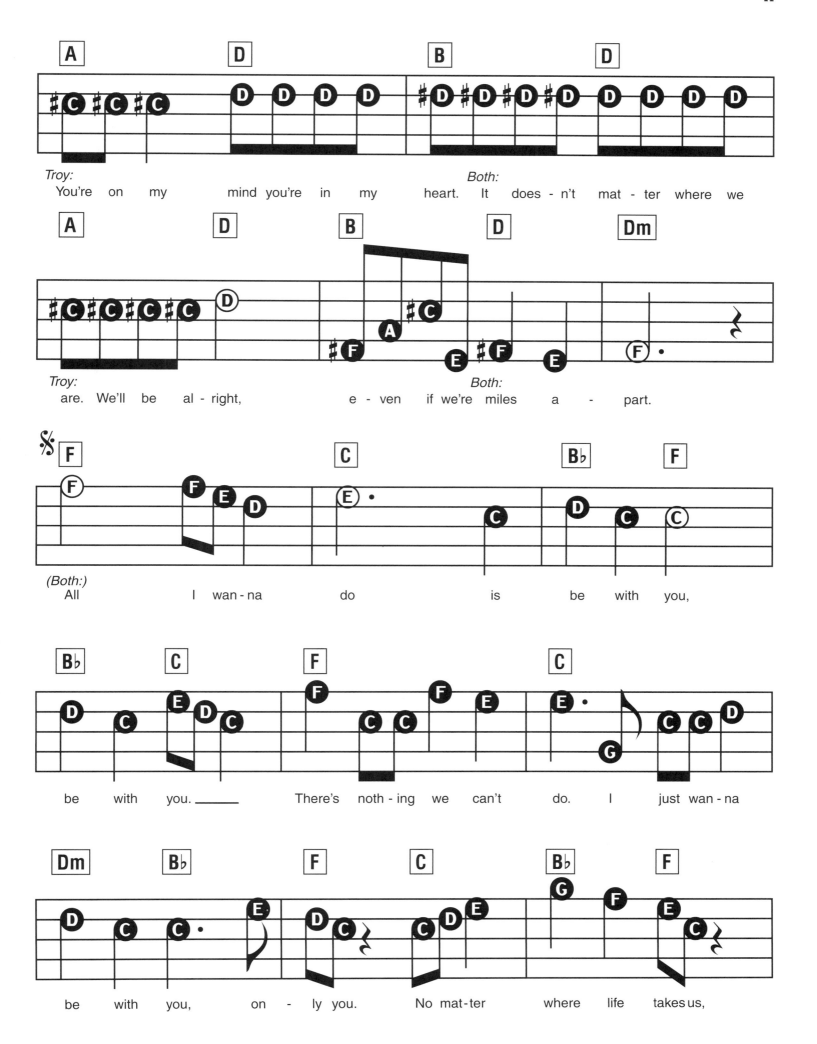

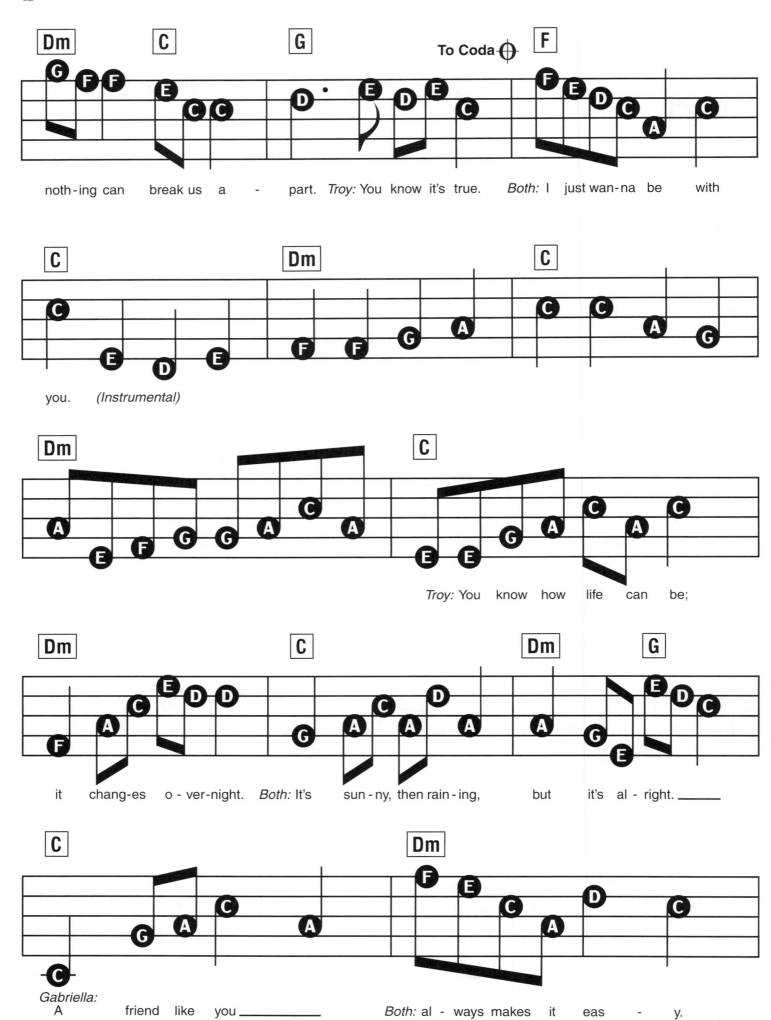

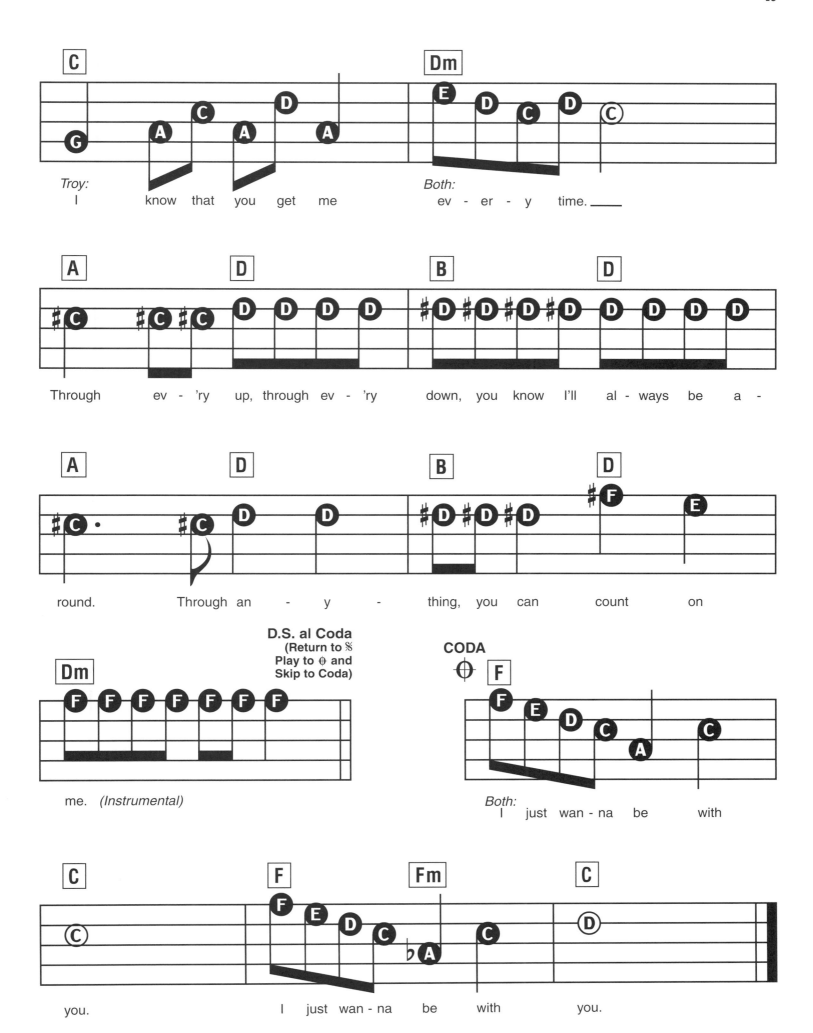

43

A Night to Remember

44

Registration 4
Rhythm: Dance or Rock

Words and Music by Matthew Gerrard
and Robbie Nevil

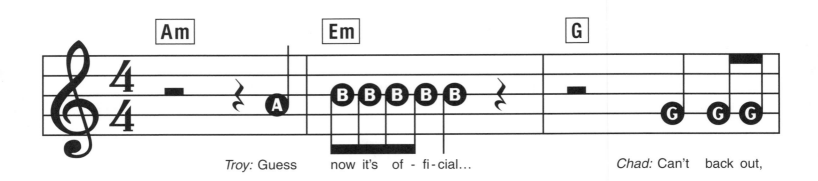

Troy: Guess now it's of-fi-cial... Chad: Can't back out,

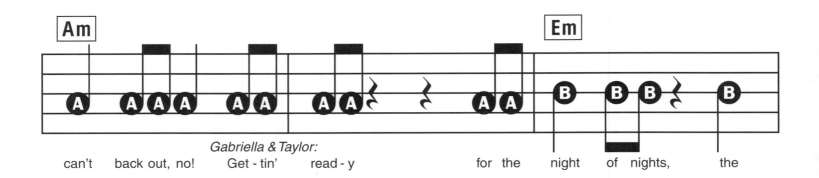

can't back out, no! Get-tin' read-y for the night of nights, the

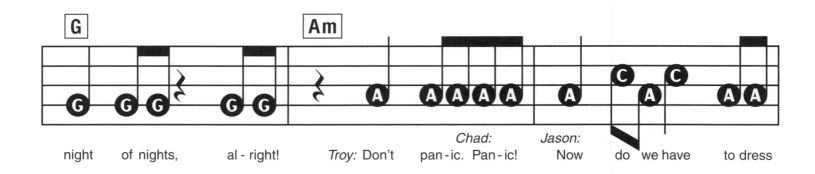

night of nights, al-right! Troy: Don't pan-ic. Pan-ic! Jason: Now do we have to dress

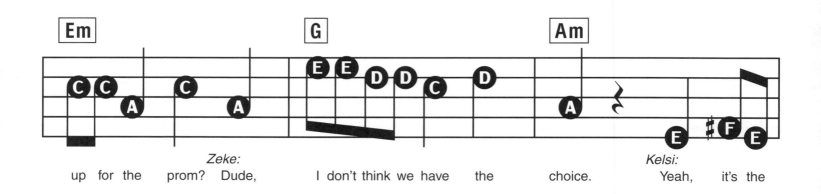

up for the prom? Dude, I don't think we have the choice. Yeah, it's the

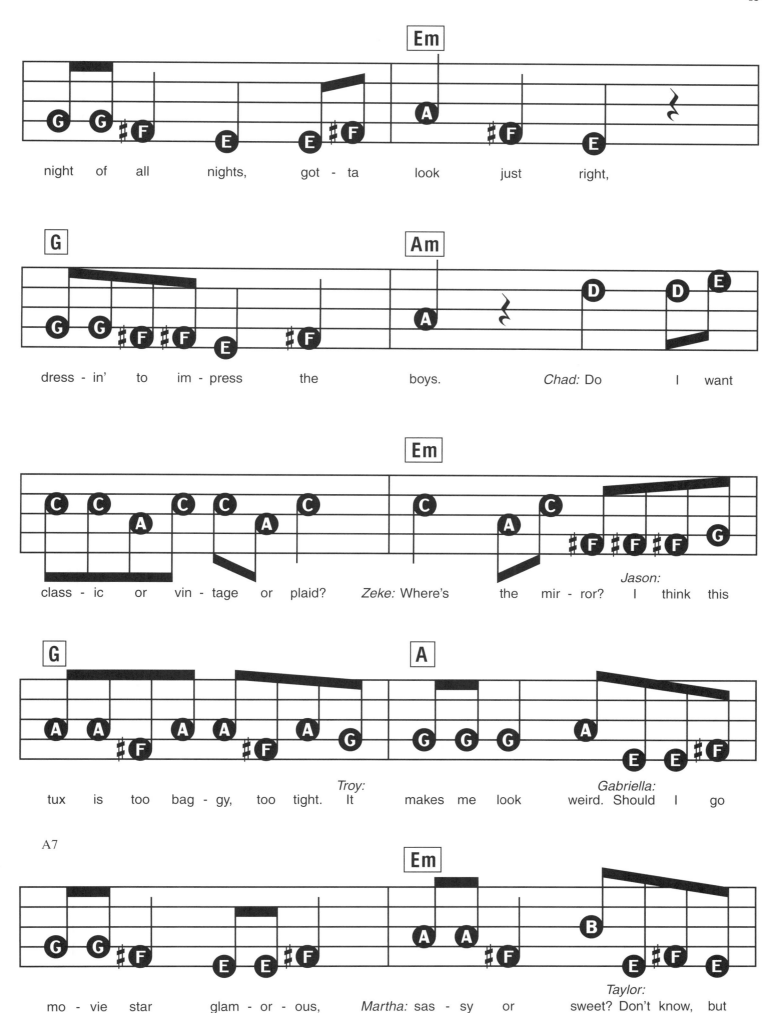

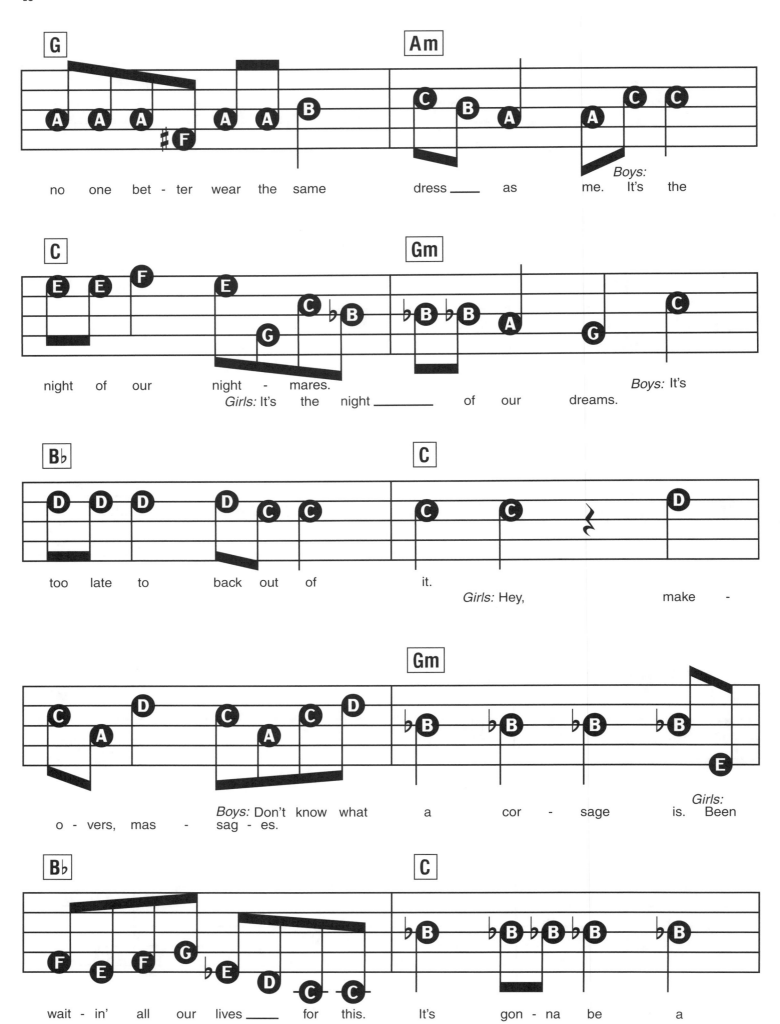

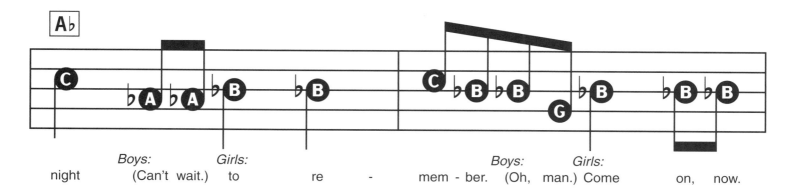

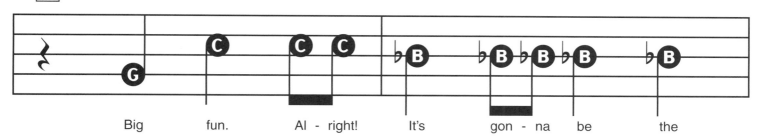

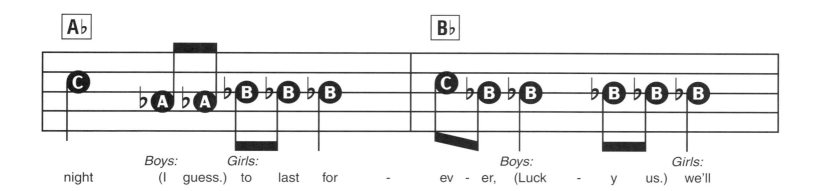

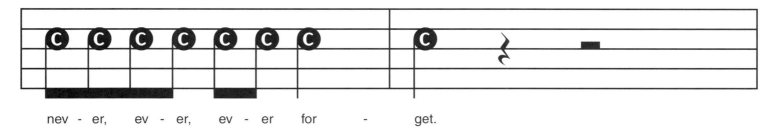

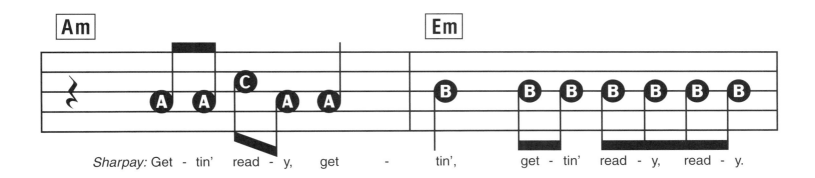

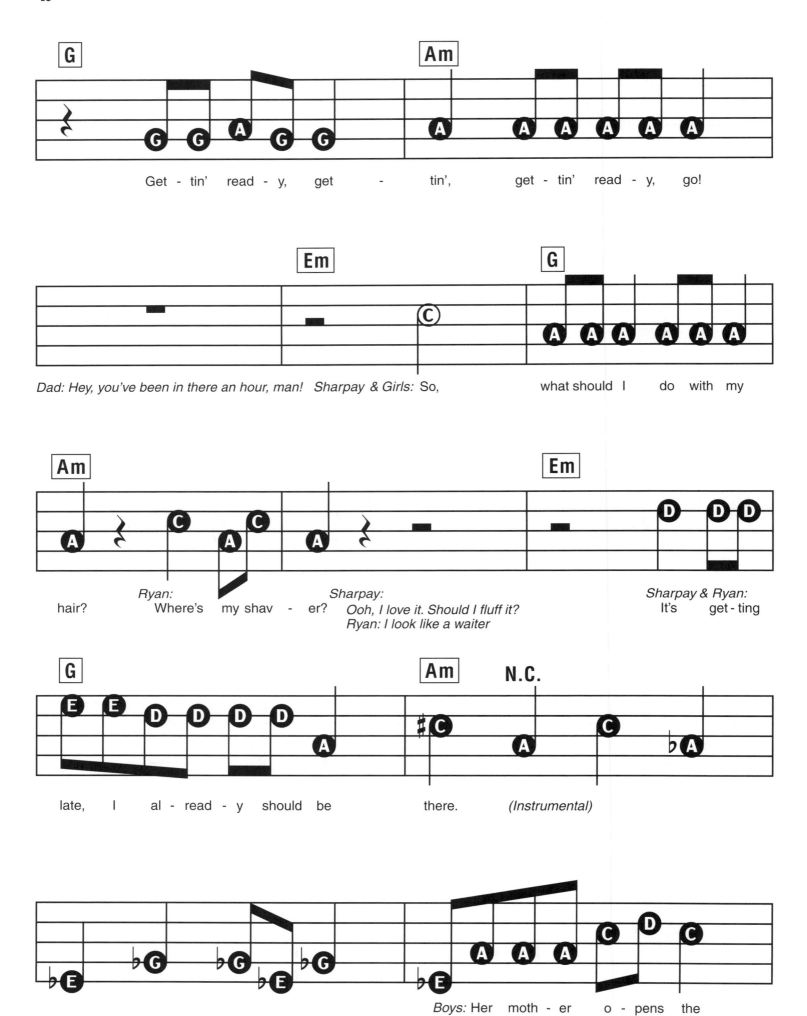

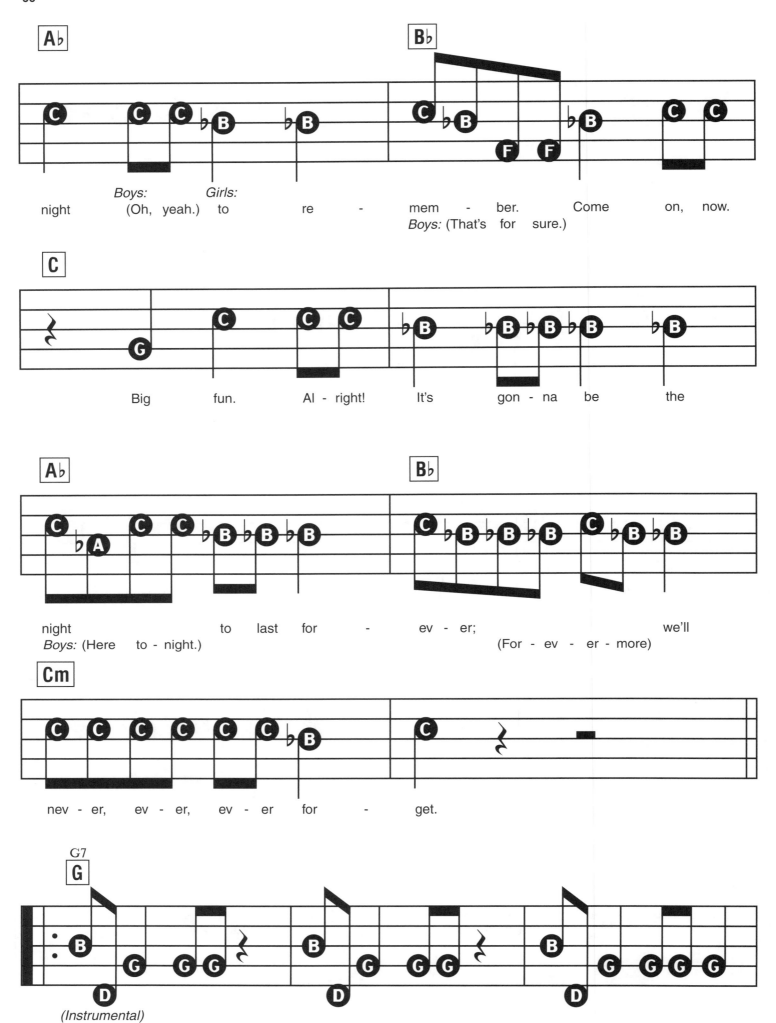

51

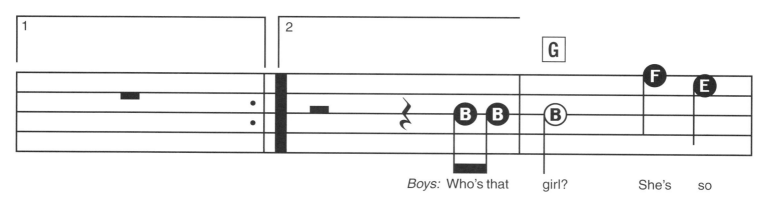
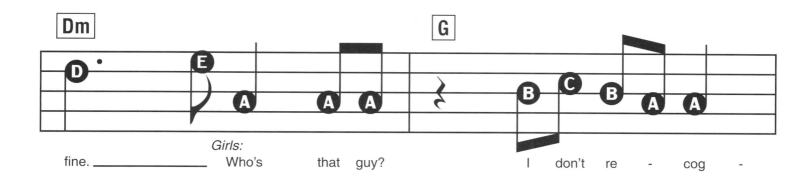
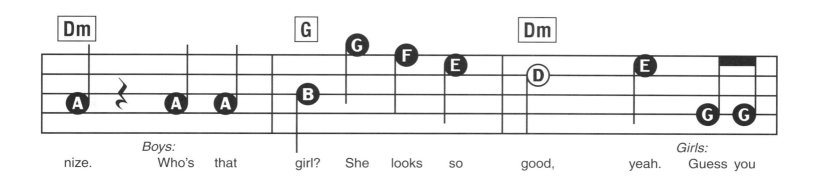
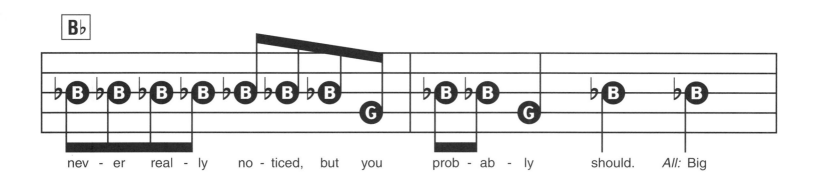
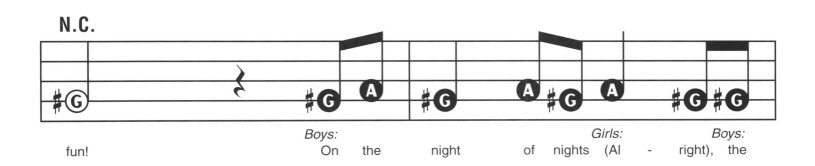

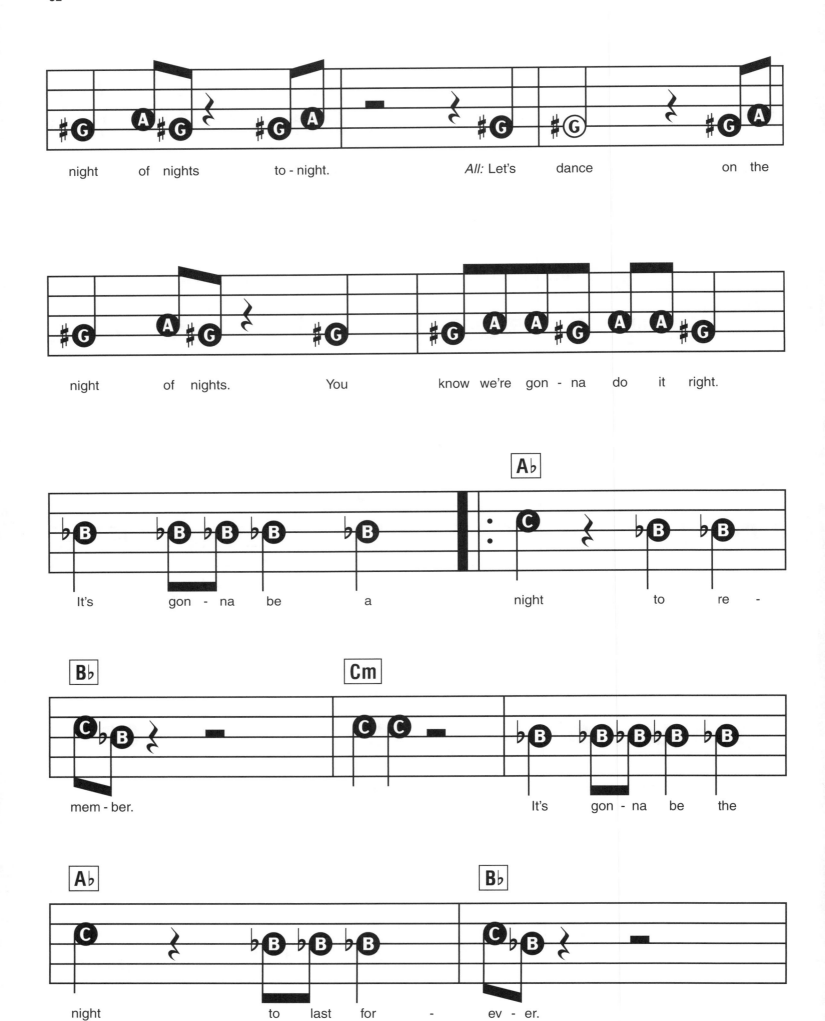

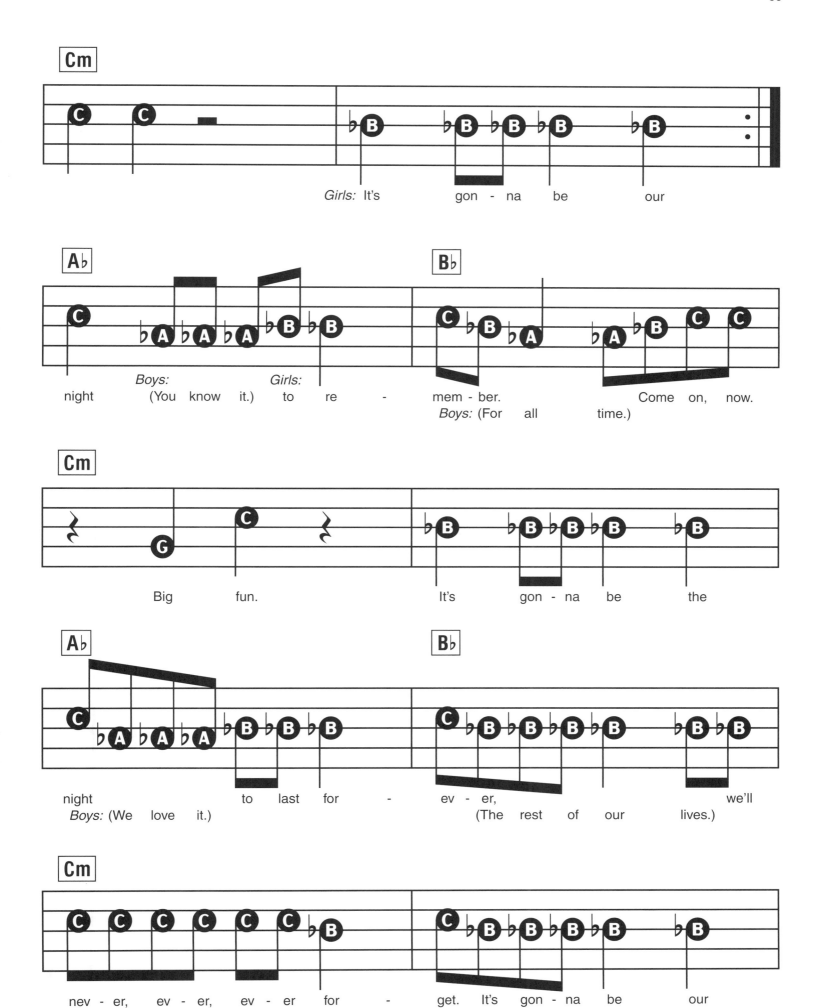

54

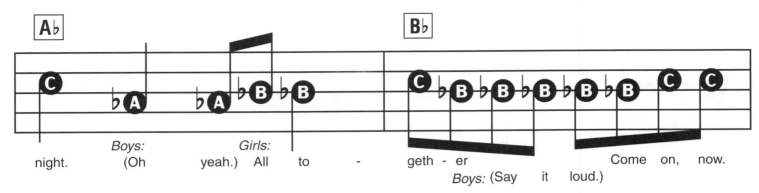

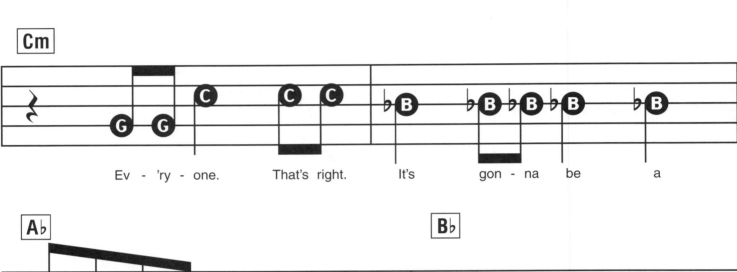

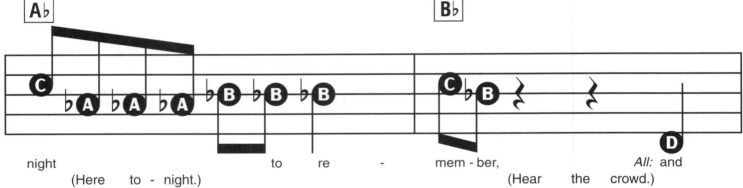

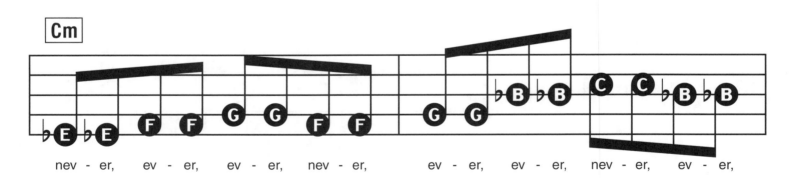

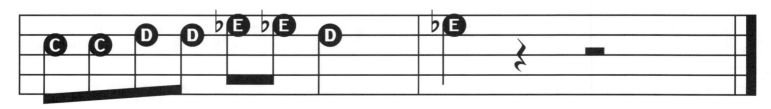

The Boys Are Back

Registration 4
Rhythm: Funk or Rock

Words and Music by Matthew Gerrard
and Robbie Nevil

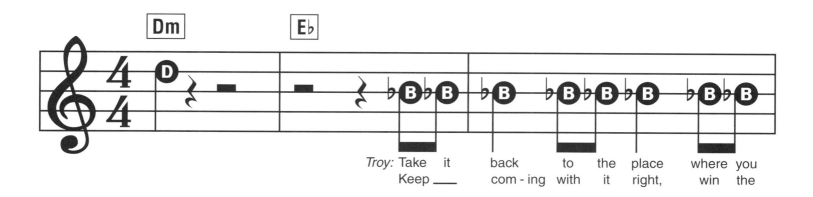

Troy: Take it back to the place where you
Keep ___ com - ing with it right, win the

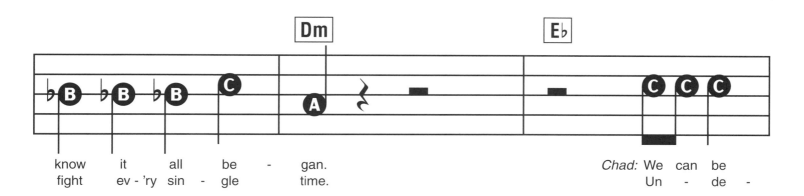

know it all be - gan.
fight ev - 'ry sin - gle time.

Chad: We can be
Un - de -

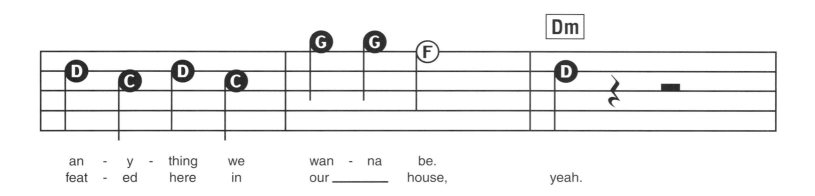

an - y - thing we wan - na be.
feat - ed here in our _____ house, yeah.

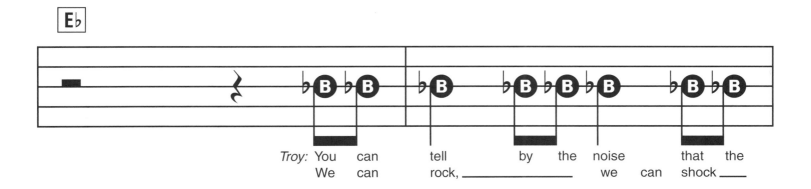

Troy: You can tell by the noise that the
We can rock, _____ we can shock ___

56

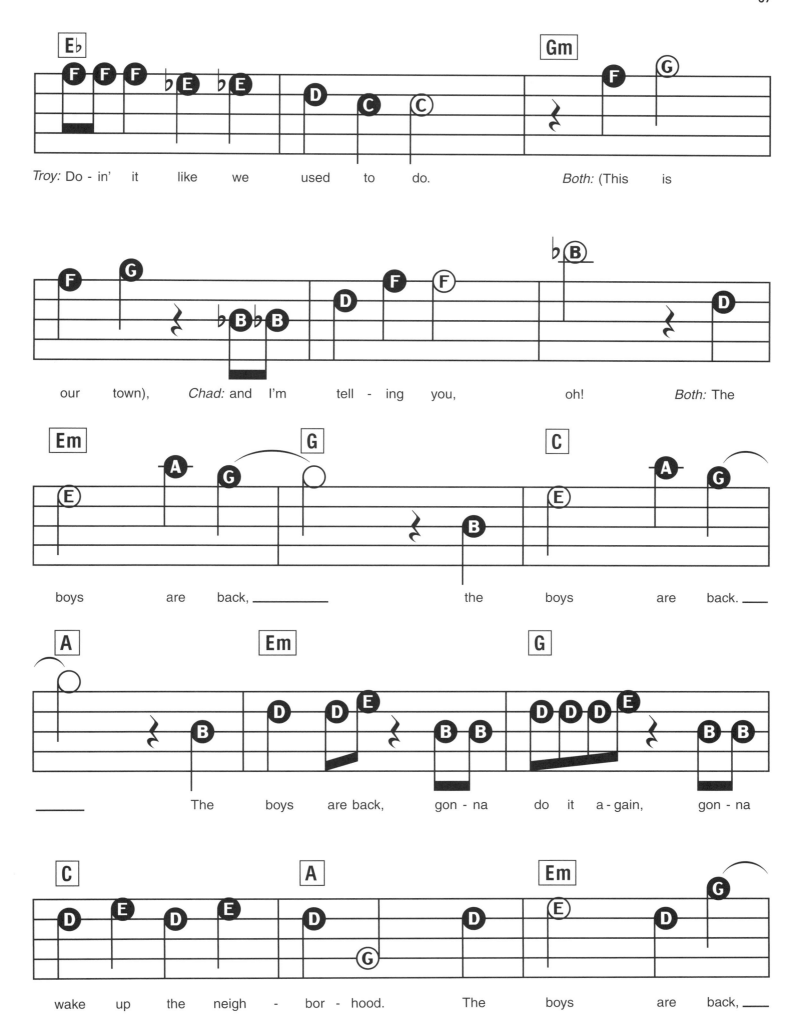

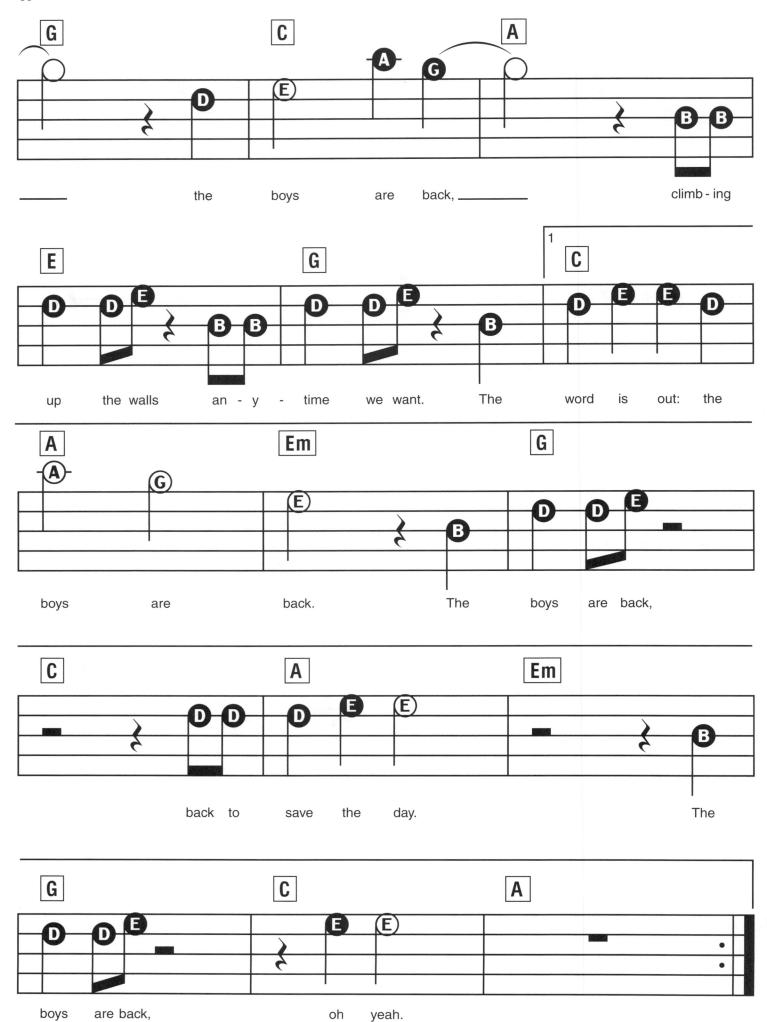

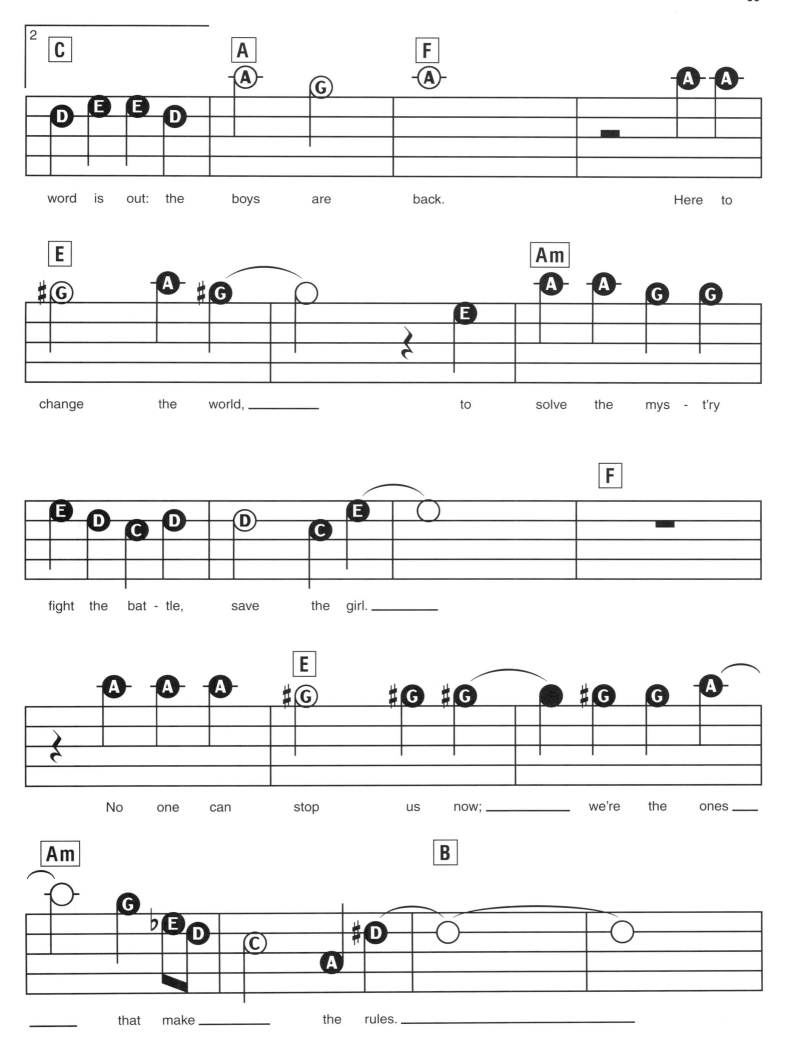

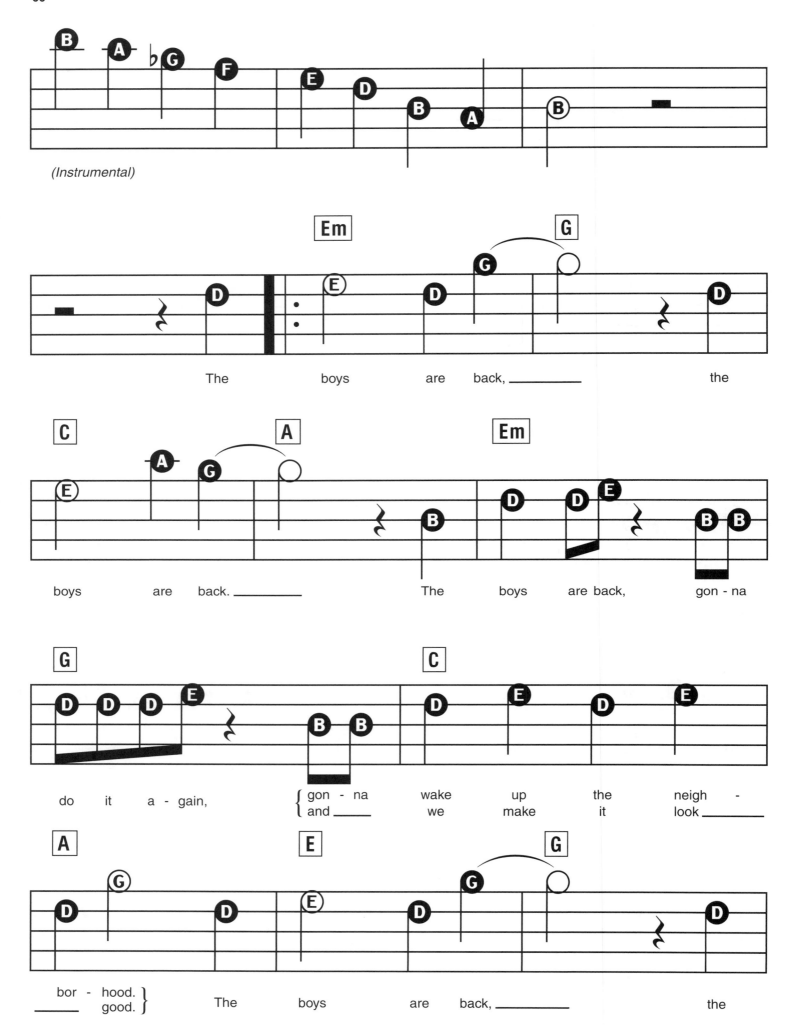

60

(Instrumental)

The   boys   are   back, _____   the

boys   are   back. _____   The   boys   are   back,   gon - na

do   it   a - gain,   { gon - na   wake   up   the   neigh -
                        and _____   we   make   it   look _____

bor - hood. }
_____ good. }   The   boys   are   back, _____   the

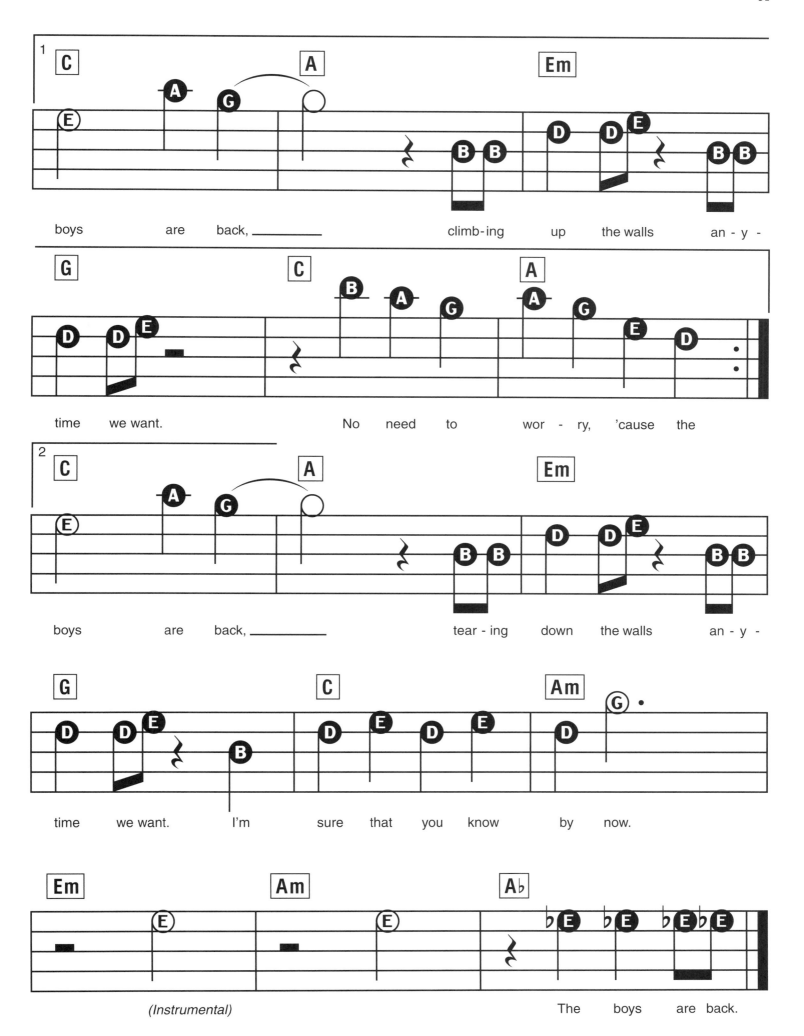

boys   are   back, _____   climb-ing   up   the   walls   an - y -

time   we want.   No   need   to   wor - ry,   'cause   the

boys   are   back, _____   tear - ing   down   the   walls   an - y -

time   we want.   I'm   sure   that   you   know   by   now.

(Instrumental)   The   boys   are   back.

Walk Away

Registration 2
Rhythm: 8 Beat or Rock

Words and Music by
Jamie Houston

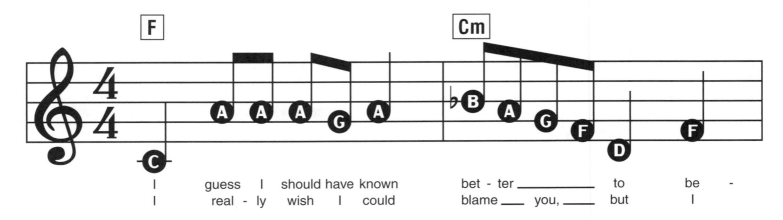

I guess I should have known bet - ter _____ to be -
I real - ly wish I could blame ___ you, ___ but I

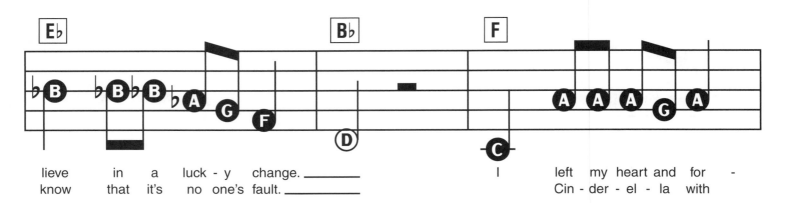

lieve in a luck - y change. _____ I left my heart and for -
know that it's no one's fault. _____ Cin - der - el - la with

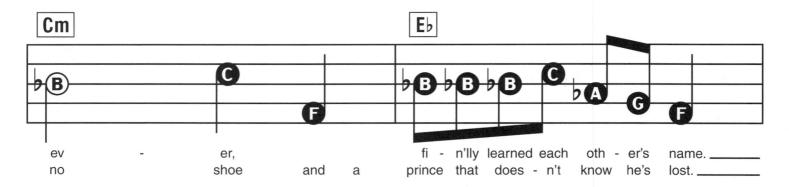

ev - er, fi - n'lly learned each oth - er's name. _____
no shoe and a prince that does - n't know he's lost. _____

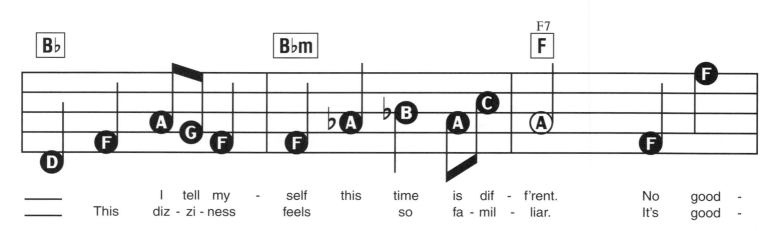

_____ I tell my - self this time is dif - f'rent. No good -
_____ This diz - zi - ness feels so fa - mil - liar. It's good -

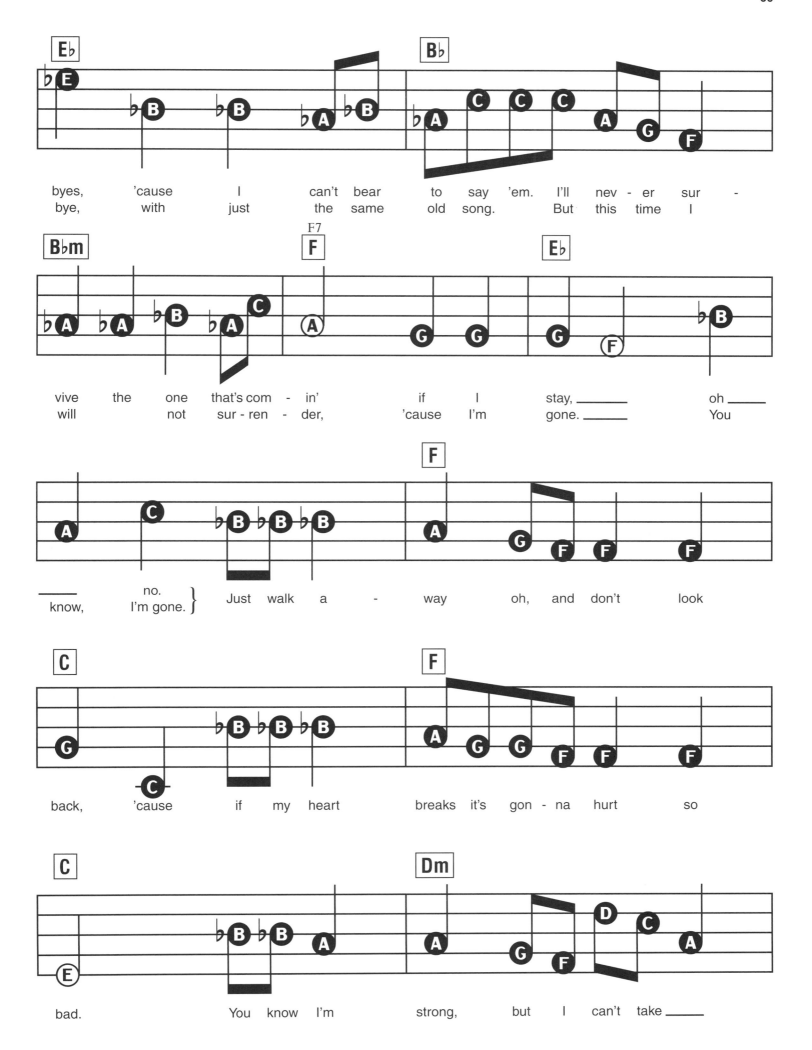

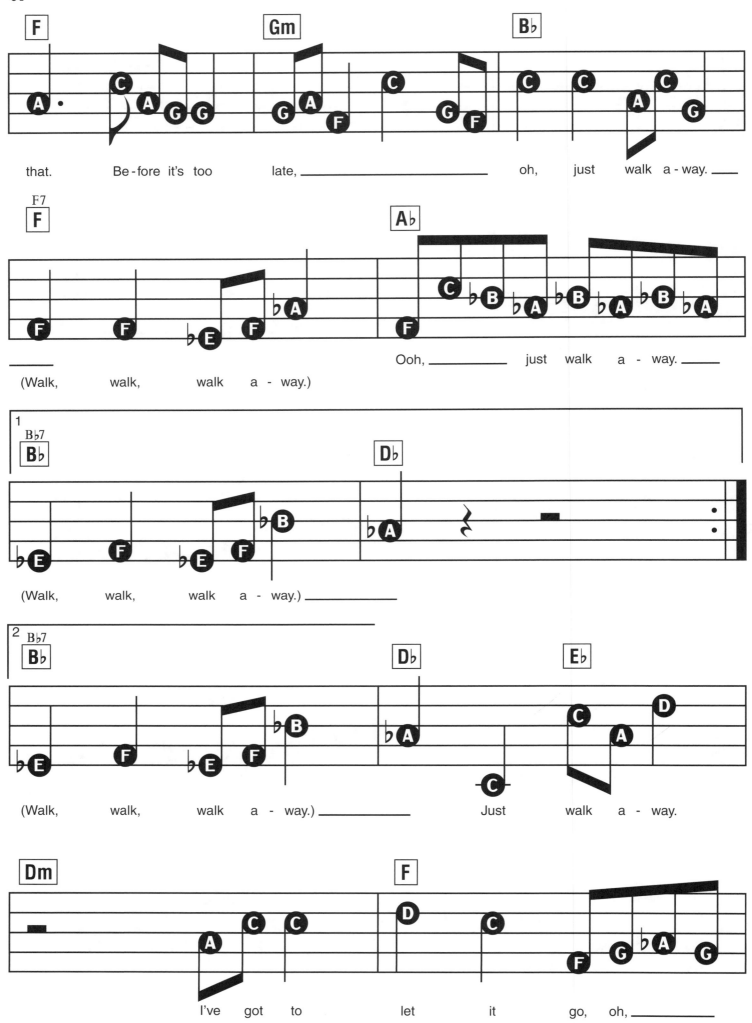

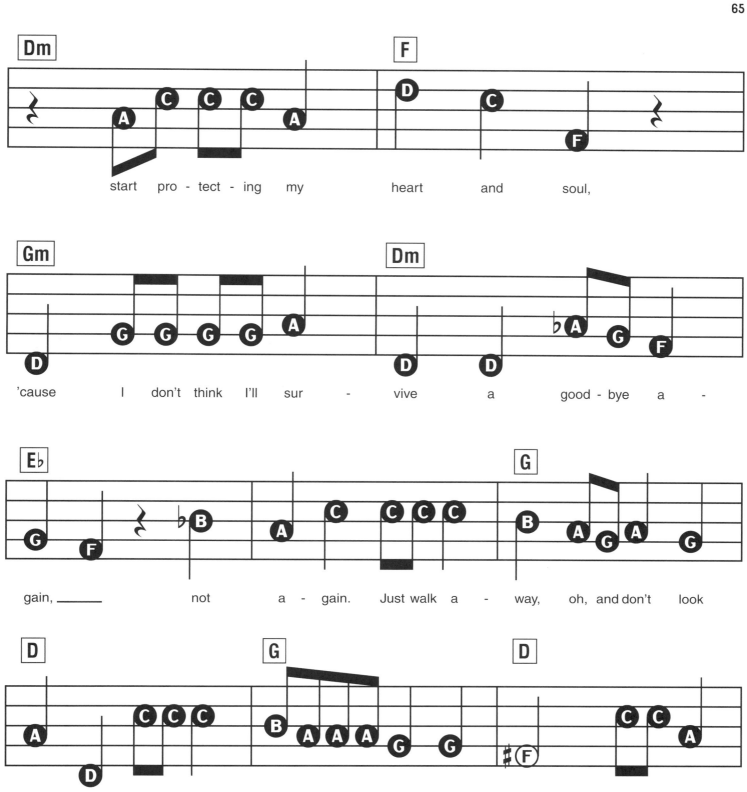

start pro - tect - ing my   heart   and   soul,

'cause   I   don't think I'll sur - vive   a   good - bye a -

gain, _____   not   a - gain. Just walk a - way, oh, and don't   look

back, cause   if my heart   breaks it's gon - na hurt   so   bad.   You know I'm

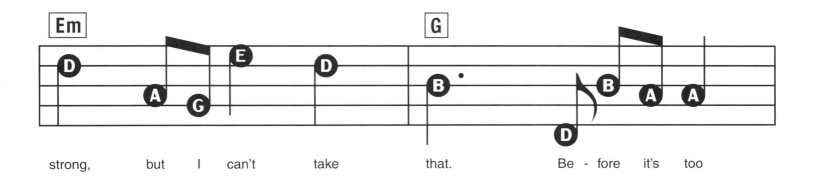

strong,   but   I can't   take   that.   Be - fore it's too

66

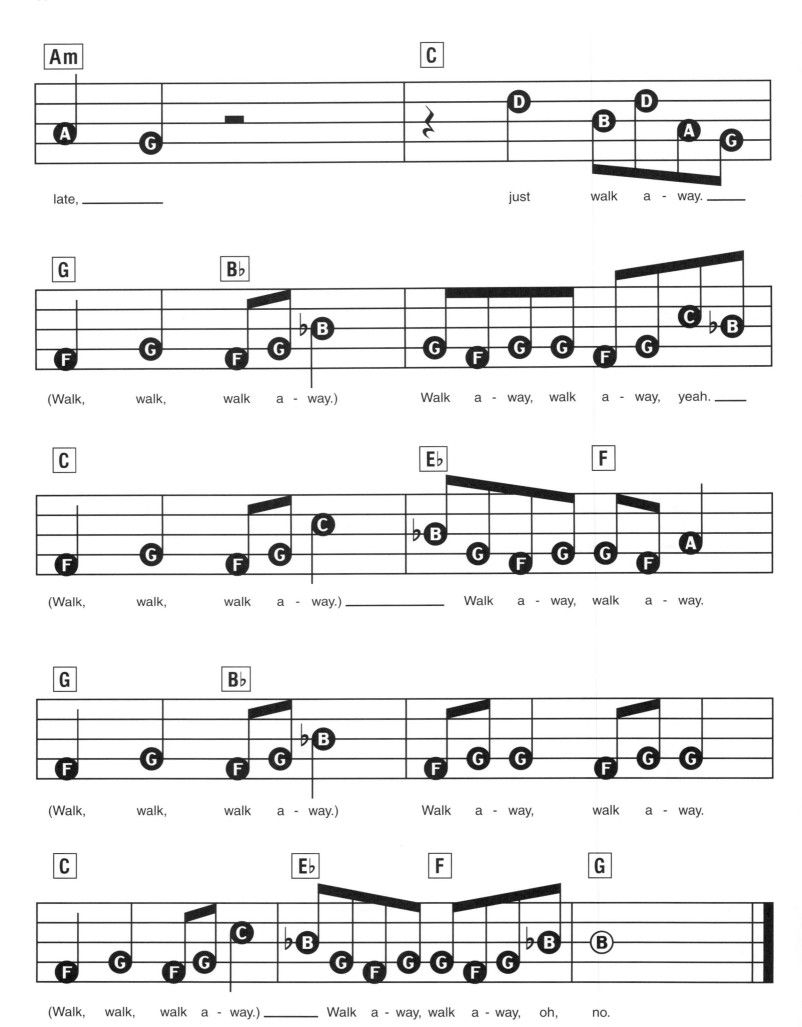

Scream

Registration 4
Rhythm: 8 Beat or Rock

Words and Music by
Jamie Houston

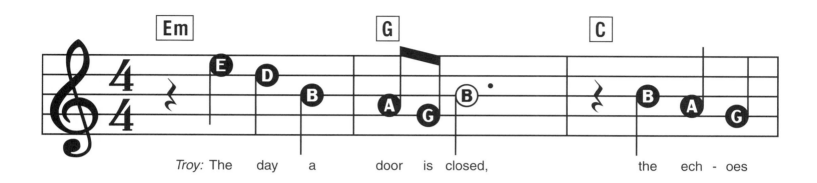

Troy: The day a door is closed, the ech - oes

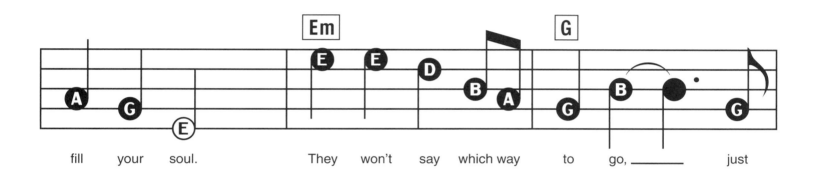

fill your soul. They won't say which way to go, _____ just

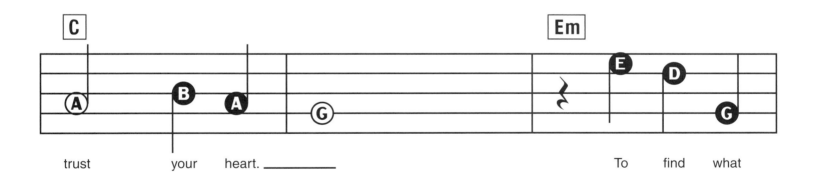

trust your heart. _____ To find what

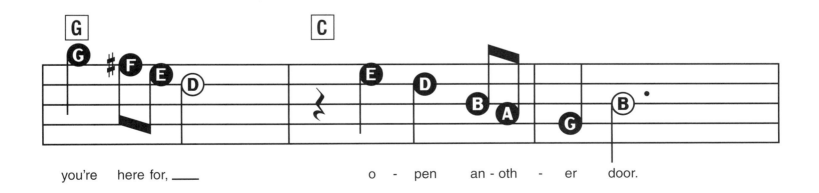

you're here for, _____ o - pen an - oth - er door.

68

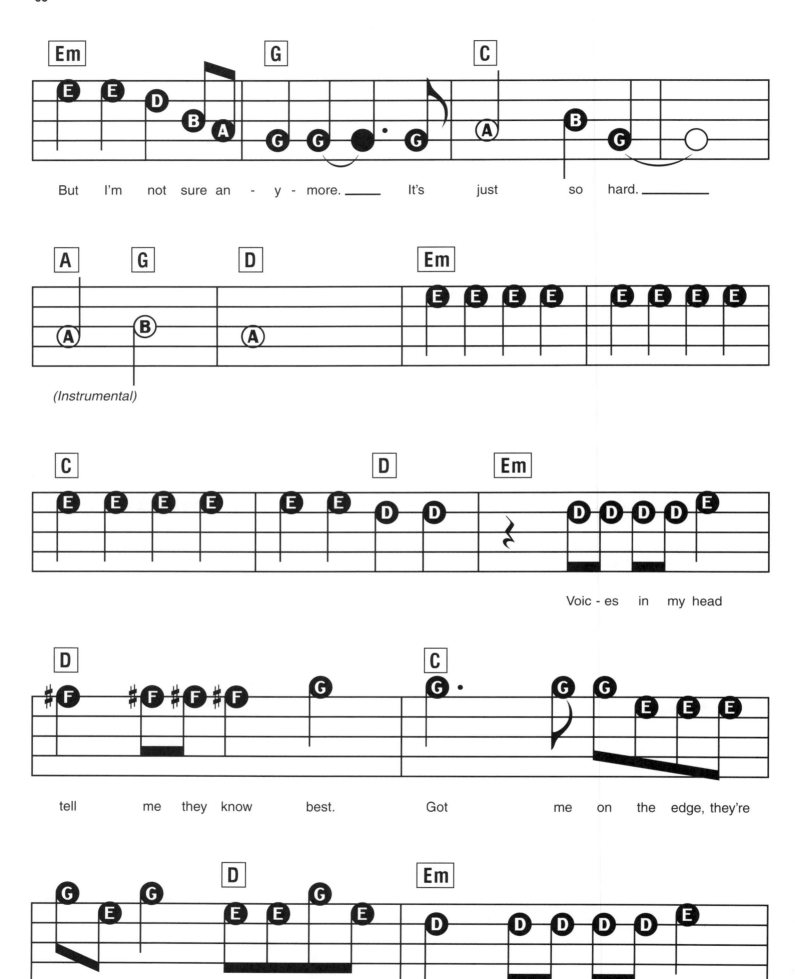

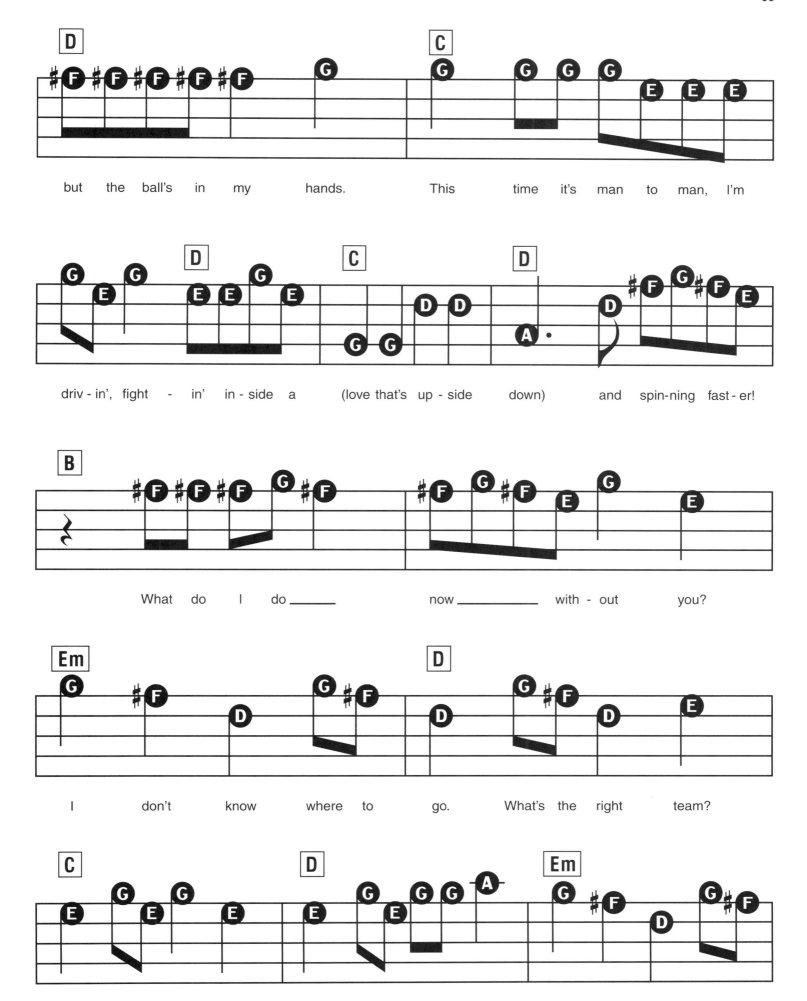

70

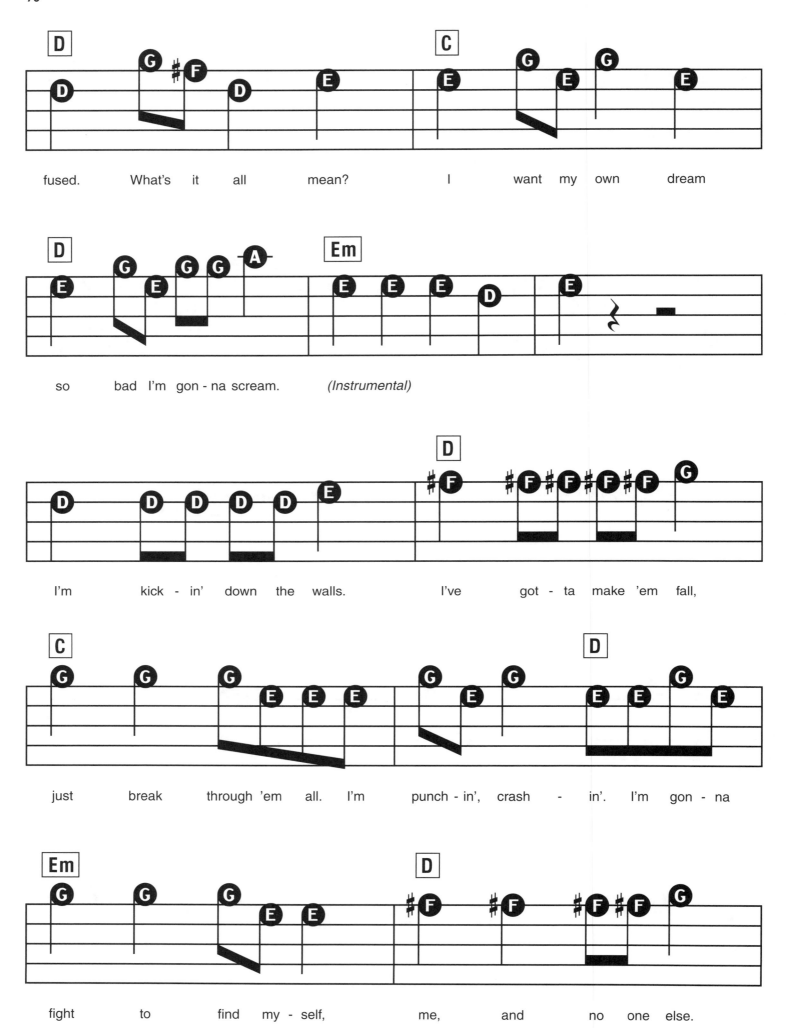

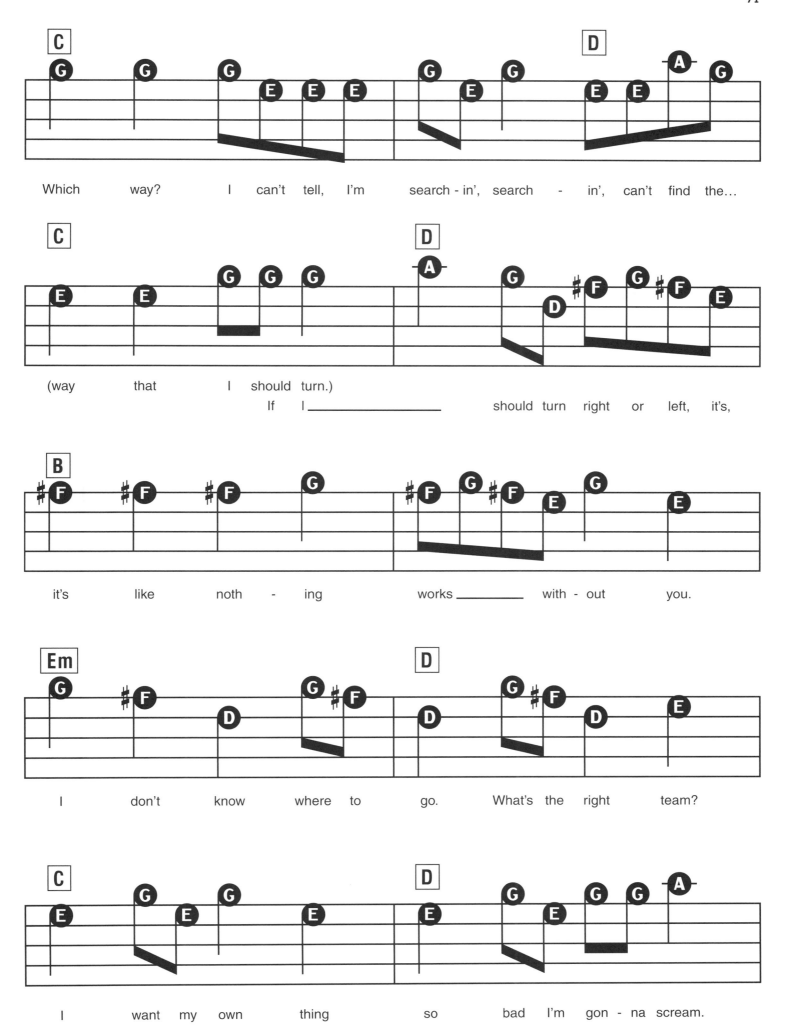

72

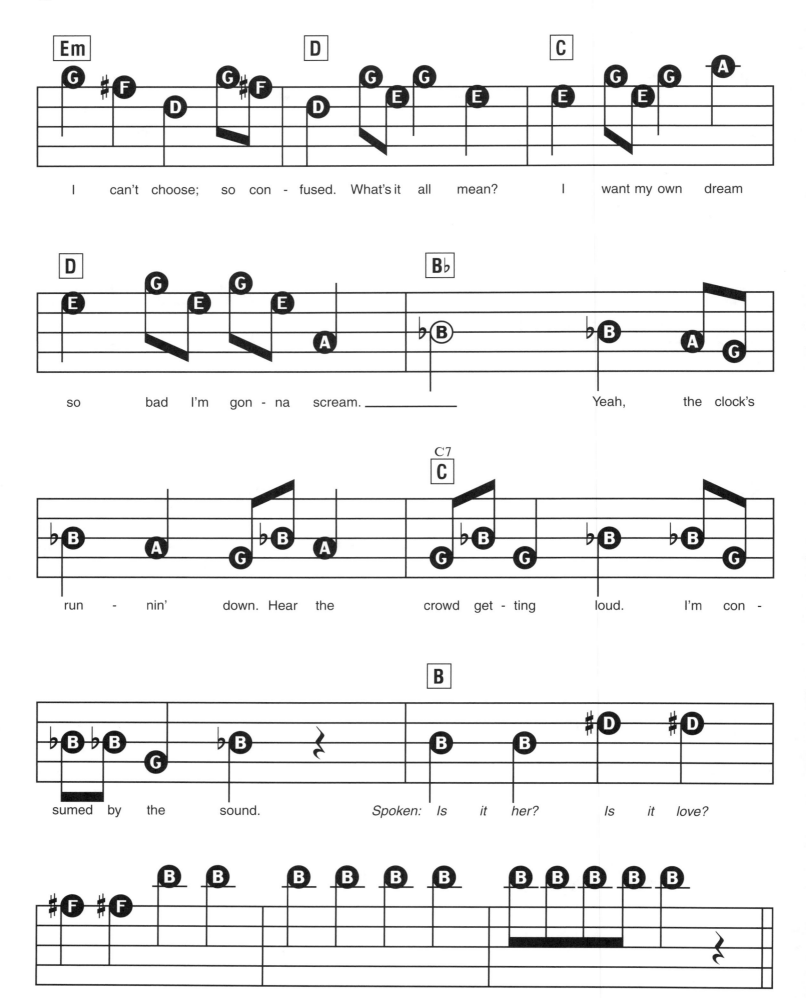

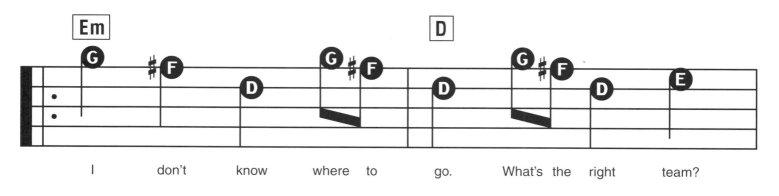

I don't know where to go. What's the right team?

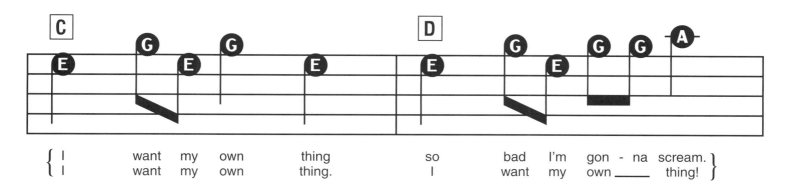

{ I want my own thing so bad I'm gon - na scream. }
{ I want my own thing. I want my own _____ thing! }

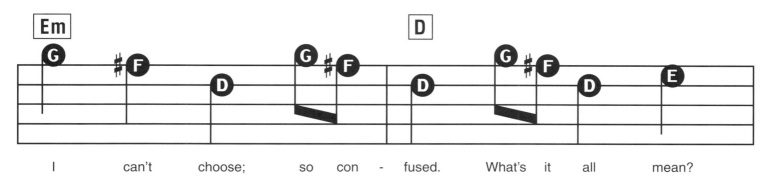

I can't choose; so con - fused. What's it all mean?

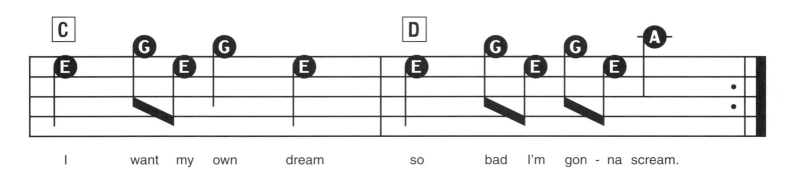

I want my own dream so bad I'm gon - na scream.

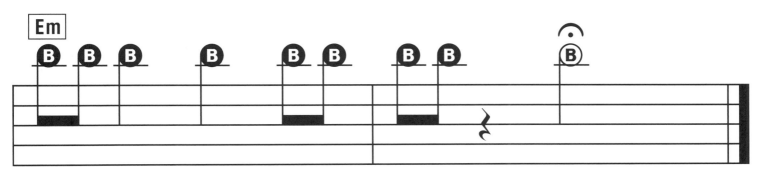

(Instrumental)   Ah!

We're All in This Together
(Graduation Version)

Registration 2
Rhythm: 4/4 Ballad or 8 Beat

Words and Music by Matthew Gerrard
and Robbie Nevil

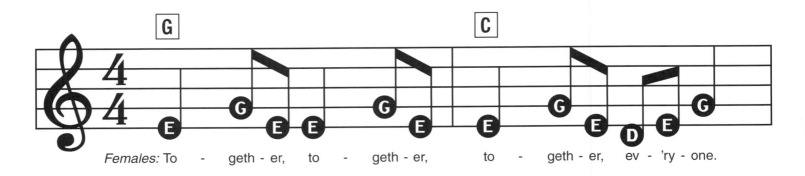

Females: To - geth - er, to - geth - er, to - geth - er, ev - 'ry - one.

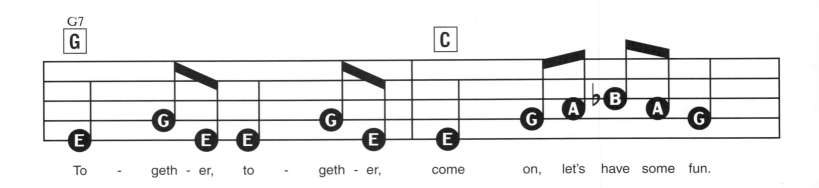

To - geth - er, to - geth - er, come on, let's have some fun.

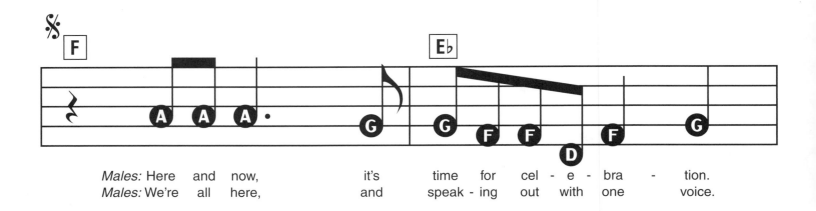

Males: Here and now, it's time for cel - e - bra - tion.
Males: We're all here, and speak - ing out with one voice.

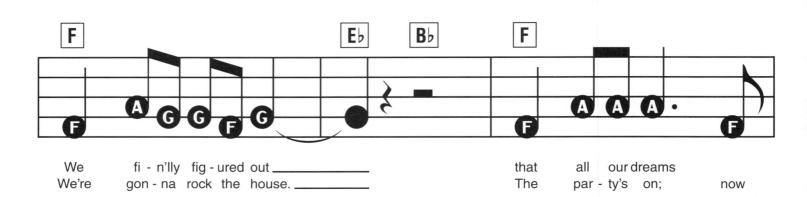

We fi - n'lly fig - ured out _____ that all our dreams
We're gon - na rock the house. _____ The par - ty's on; now

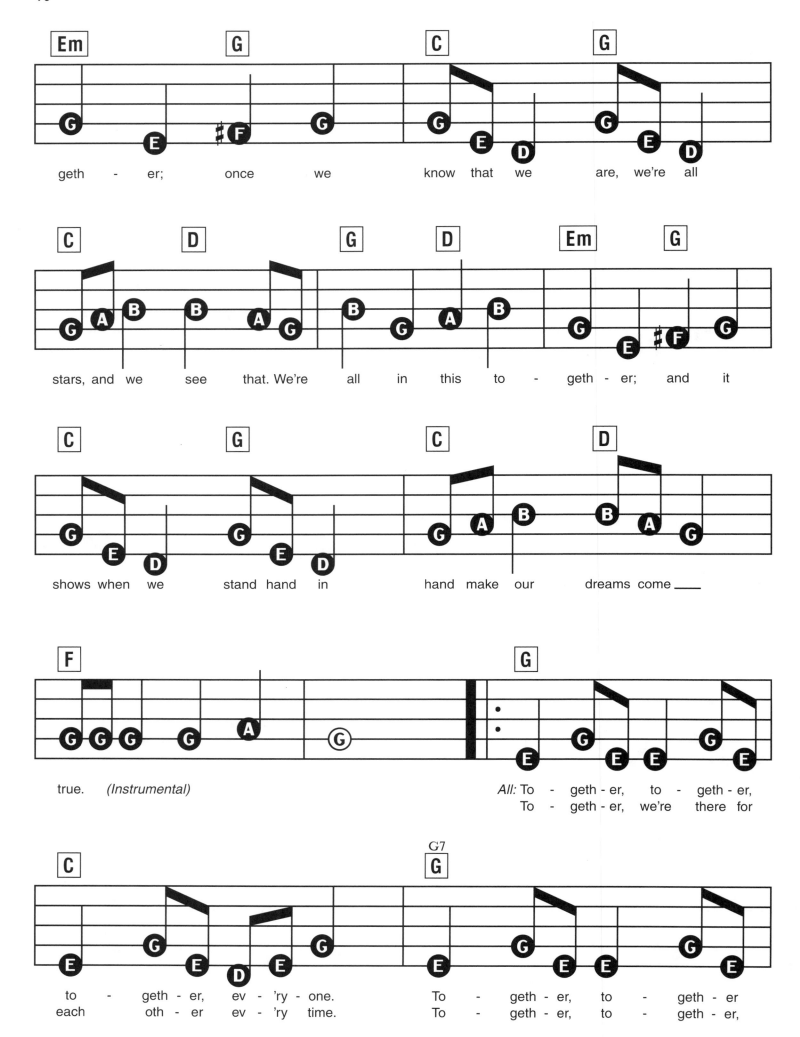

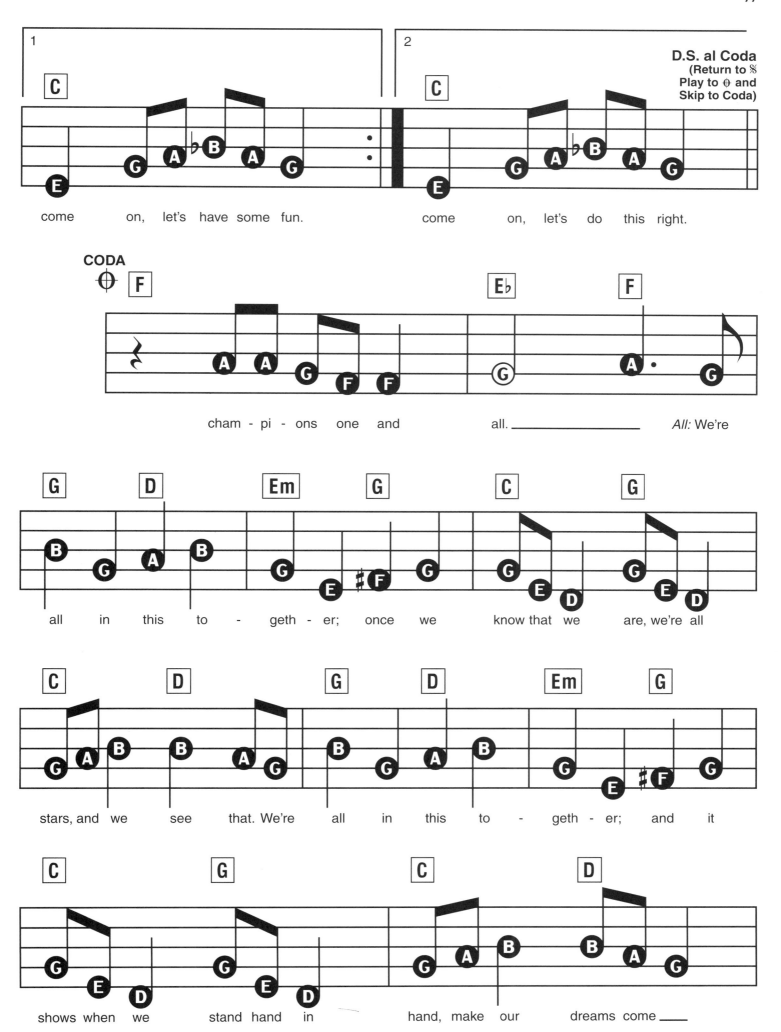

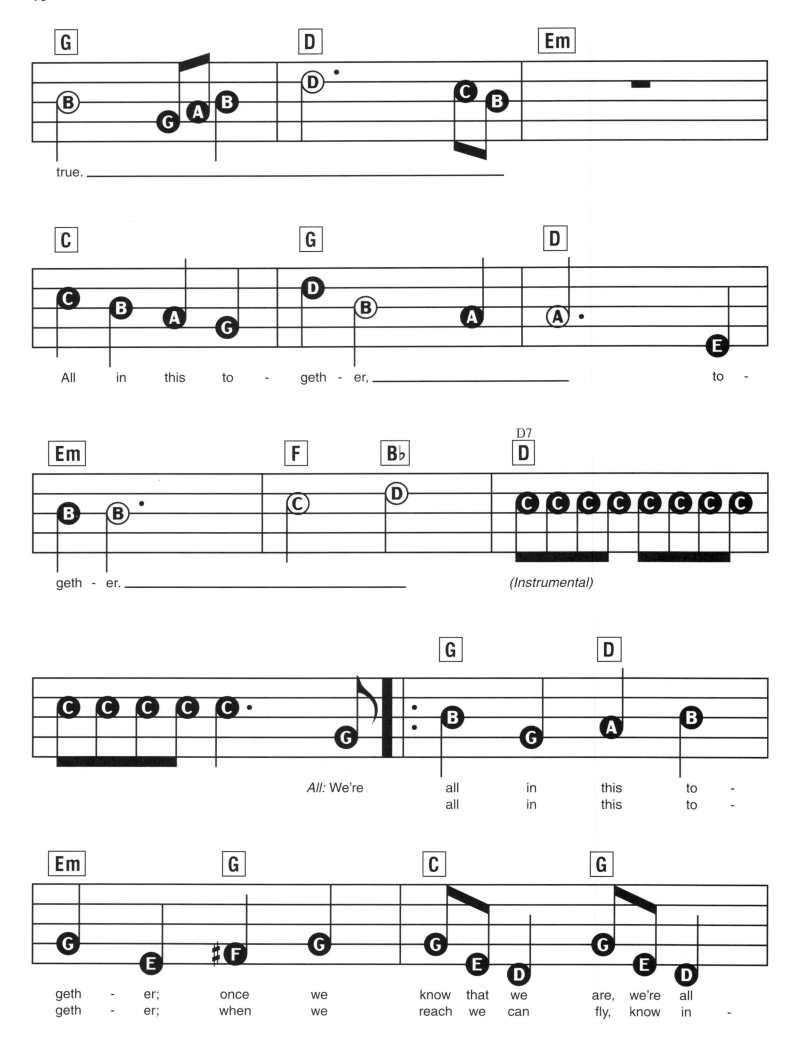

High School Musical

Registration 4
Rhythm: Dance or Rock

Words and Music by Matthew Gerrard
and Robbie Nevil

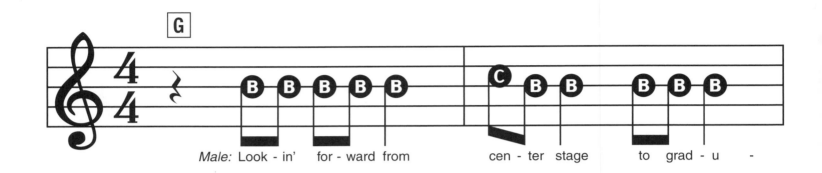

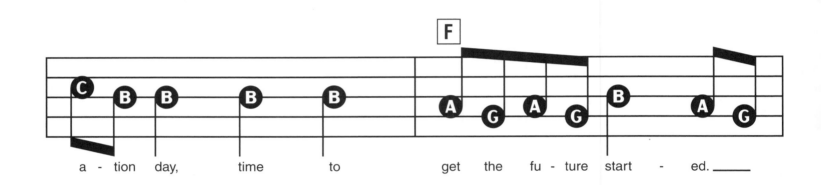

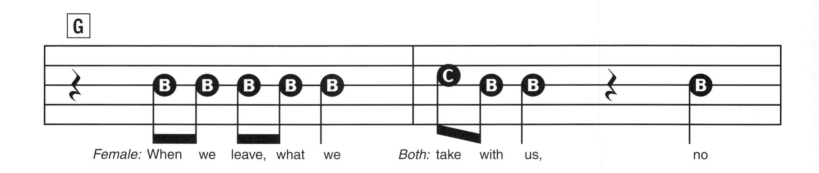

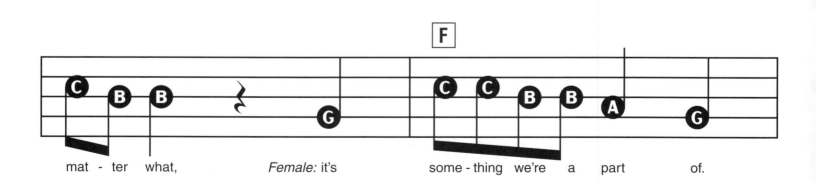

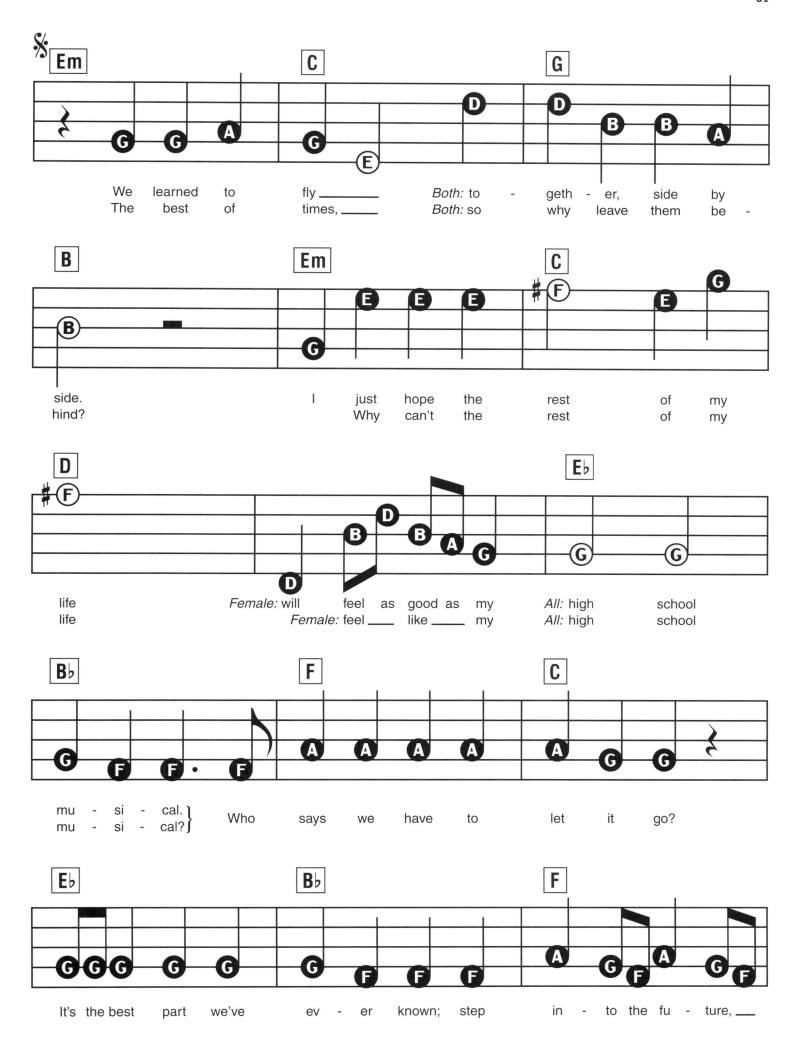

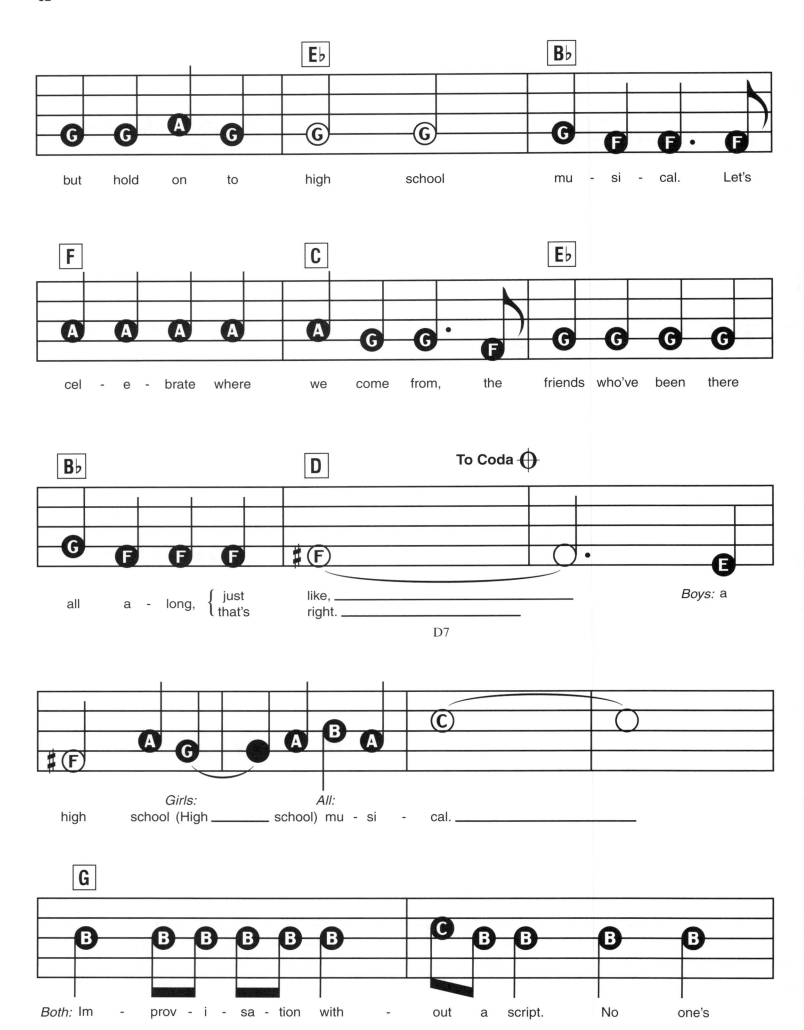

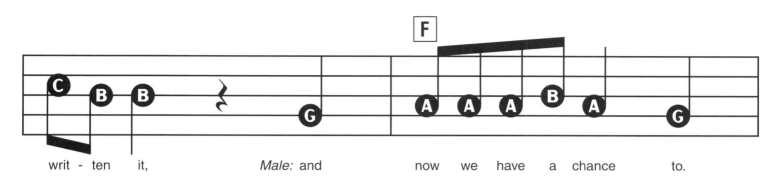

writ - ten it, *Male:* and now we have a chance to.

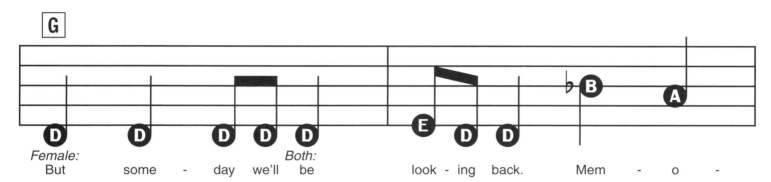

Female: But some - day we'll be *Both:* look - ing back. Mem - o -

D.S. al Coda
(Return to ℅
Play to ⊕ and
Skip to Coda)

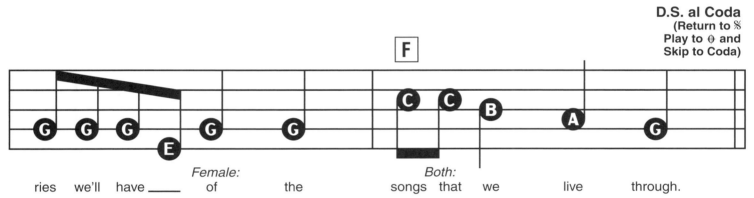

ries we'll have ____ *Female:* of the *Both:* songs that we live through.

CODA

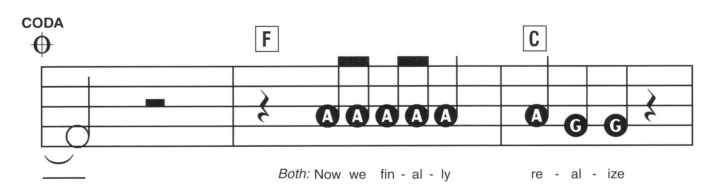

Both: Now we fin - al - ly re - al - ize

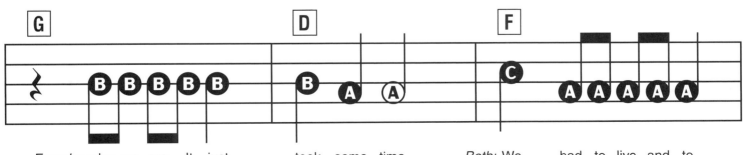

Female: who we are. It just took some time. *Both:* We had to live, and to

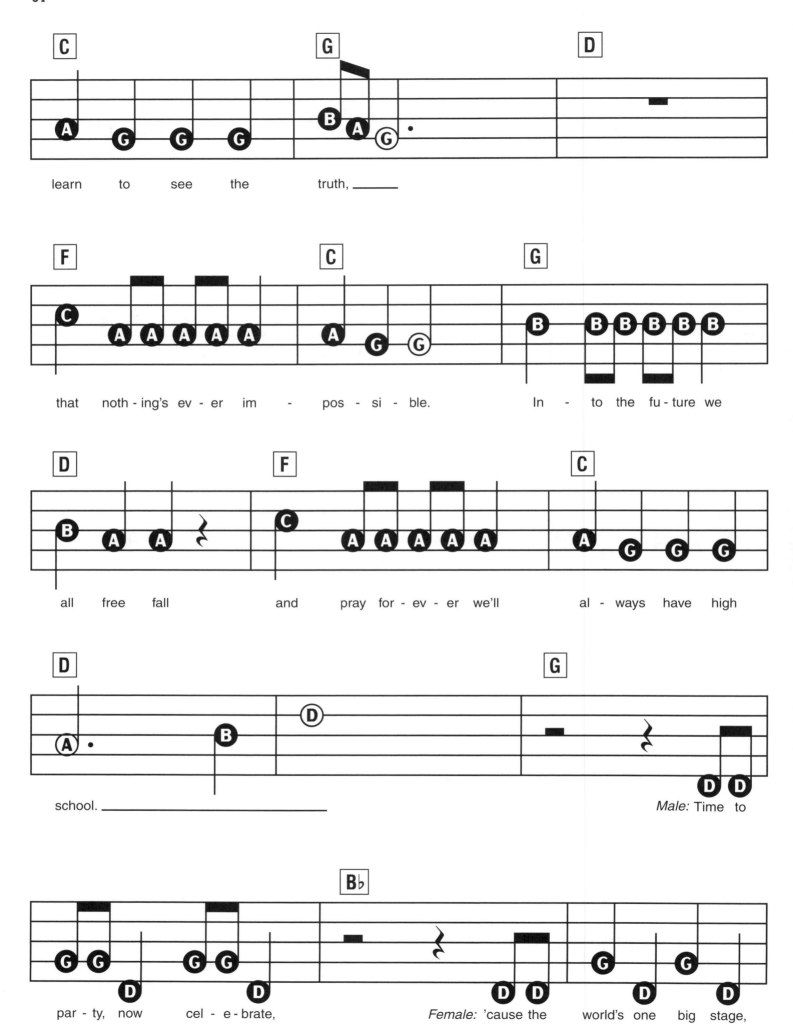

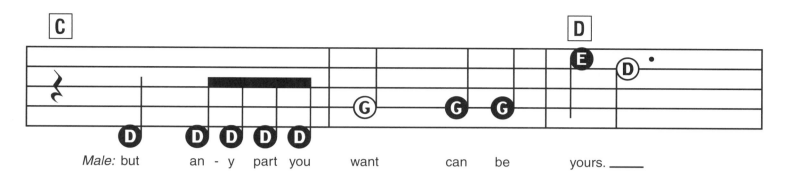

C

Male: but an - y part you want can be yours. _____

D

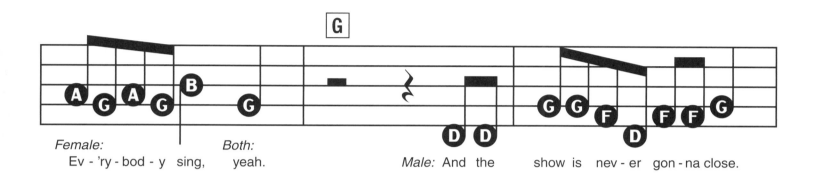

Female: Ev - 'ry - bod - y sing, yeah.

Both:

G

Male: And the show is nev - er gon - na close.

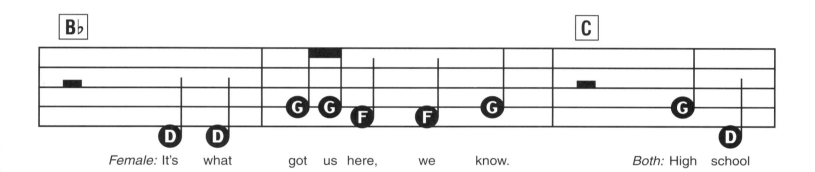

B♭

Female: It's what got us here, we know.

C

Both: High school

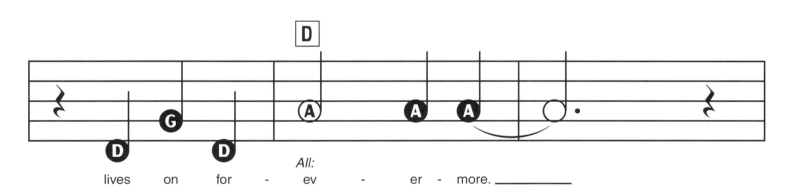

D

All:
lives on for - ev - er - more. _____

D7

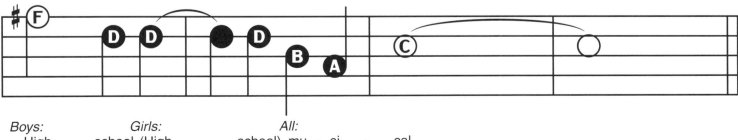

Boys: Girls: All:
High school (High _____ school) mu - si - cal. _____

86

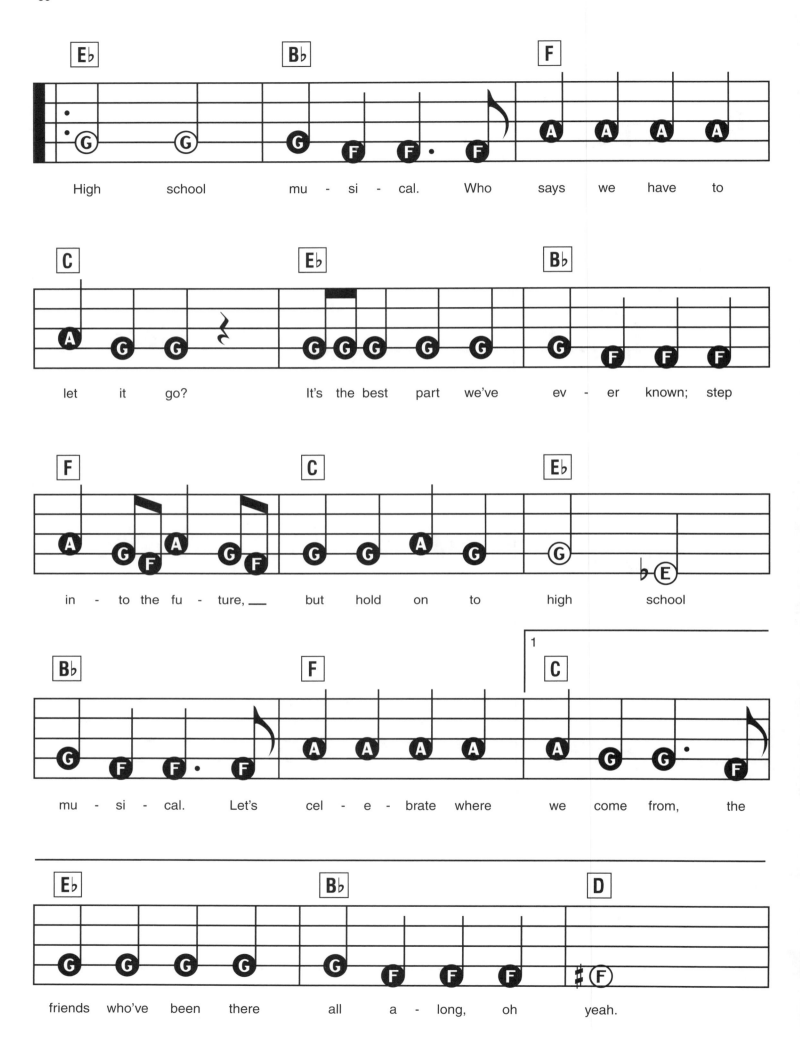